Praise for *Faith Beyond Borders*

"*Faith Beyond Borders* shows in one dramatic story after another the power of compassionate action by peacemakers. I have known Don and Carolyn Mosley and their community of Jubilee Partners for many years. They have discovered repeatedly that when we reach out to others in love, we find that God is right there with us in the effort. I urge people of goodwill everywhere to read this book and be inspired."
—**Jimmy Carter**

"Don Mosley believes that when Jesus told us to love our enemies and to welcome the stranger, he really meant it. From Jubilee Partners, a place of hospitality for thousands of refugees from dozens of countries, to Habitat for Humanity International, transforming building houses into missions of reconciliation, he has lived a faith that indeed goes beyond borders. It is a book that will move you to tears and stir you to action."
—**Jim Wallis,** President of Sojourners and author of *Rediscovering Values*

"Increasingly, there are Christians who are concluding that Jesus meant what he said in the Sermon on the Mount, and they are trying to live out Christ's teachings. Don Mosley is one of them, and in this book he shares with us what a follower of Christ looks like in the 21st century."
—**Tony Campolo,** author of *Choose Love, Not Power*

"Don Mosley takes us beyond the borders of our limited imaginations to catch a little glimpse of the life that's possible when we take Jesus at his word. Don is a great storyteller—and this is a book full of great stories—but, more than that, Don is someone who dives into God's Story with his whole life. We've learned a wealth of wisdom from him. Hope you will too."

—**Shane Claiborne** and **Jonathan Wilson-Hartgrove,** authors of *Becoming the Answer to Our Prayers*

"Let us give thanks for this noble and searing book, and for all who regard high walls as mere cobwebs hung on thin air by irksome children, to be brushed aside purposefully, with a smile. The implicit motto is celebrated on page after page: When we behave humanly, living beyond the walls and borders, wonders will follow."

—**Daniel Berrigan,** author of *No Gods But One*

FAITH BEYOND BORDERS

doing justice in a dangerous world

Don Mosley
with JOYCE HOLLYDAY

To Gail,

Don

June 27, 2010

Abingdon Press
Nashville

FAITH BEYOND BORDERS
DOING JUSTICE IN A DANGEROUS WORLD

Copyright © 2010 by Abingdon Press

This book is printed on acid-free paper.

Library of Congress Cataloging-in-Publication Data

Mosley, Don, 1939-
  Faith beyond borders : doing justice in a dangerous world / by Don Mosley with Joyce Hollyday.
    p. cm.
  Includes bibliographical references (p.   ).
  ISBN 978-1-4267-0789-6 (binding: pbk./trade pbk., adhesive-perfect binding : alk. paper)
    1. Church work with refugees—Georgia—Comer. 2. Mosley, Don, 1939- 3. Jubilee Partners. I. Hollyday, Joyce. II. Title.
  BV4466.M668 2010
  261.8′32809758152—dc22

                                                                                    2010002642

10 11 12 13 14 15 16 17 18 19—10 9 8 7 6 5 4 3 2 1

MANUFACTURED IN THE UNITED STATES OF AMERICA

Dedicated to the memory of Millard Fuller,

my dear brother who taught me that when we

pray sincerely for God to lead us in a work of compassion,

we'd better get ready to do some running!

Contents

Foreword ix

Acknowledgments xiii

Introduction xv

1. Building on Solid Rock. 1

2. But I Say Unto You 17

3. No Time to Waste 43

4. Aid and Comfort 55

5. I'm Not Lost from God 73

6. Stars in the East 95

7. Groundbreaking Faith 119

Epilogue: Action and Reaction 133

Notes 141

Foreword

Have you ever been so completely spellbound by a film that you felt glued to your seat, even after the credits? Well, that was how *Faith Beyond Borders* affected me. The story is dramatic and inspiring. As one fascinating adventure followed another, I could barely stop reading. Knowing Don Mosley, that shouldn't have surprised me.

My husband Millard Fuller and I became acquainted with Don in 1970 at a Christian community in southwest Georgia called Koinonia Farm. Over the years, Don has continued to be a close friend and coworker through many struggles. I know him to be one of the most courageous, faith-driven men of our times, and yet we also have enjoyed simple pleasures together such as breaking bread, hiking to mountaintops, and having long, meaningful conversations. Love and peace run deep within the core of this man.

Don Mosley reminds me of the main character Don Quixote in the Broadway musical *Man of La Mancha*—"willing to march into hell for a heavenly cause." I discovered in this book just how many such "heavenly causes" Don has pursued. For him, there is no trip too far and no job too difficult if he is convinced that God has called him to it.

Times with Don are vividly etched in my memory. In 1974, Millard and I were missionaries living in the middle of Africa, testing out the partnership housing model that was to become Habitat for Humanity. A large parcel of land had been donated by the government of Zaire for the construction of at least one hundred houses, and we needed a surveyor. Millard remembered his "engineer buddy" still living at Koinonia and wrote him a letter. Don responded affirmatively and said he could join us in a couple of weeks. If I close my eyes I can still remember Don's arrival, his hand waving in the distance as the stern wheeler transport barge slowly approached us on the Congo River. Then, despite three-digit temperatures, he worked at breakneck speed among the trees and giant termite hills to lay out the first project so we could begin building houses.

Another time, in the early 1980s, Don was riding with Millard and me from Atlanta to Americus, Georgia, where Habitat's first headquarters was located. We were looking for a place to eat, and Don let us know that he preferred "mom and pop" fare. We passed fast-food places one after another. I thought I would starve to death before we finally spotted "Betty's Diner"!

I remember enjoying meals at Jubilee Partners, the Christian service community in Comer, Georgia, that was formed by Don and others from Koinonia. (Don, signing on as cook at breakfast, took pride in his whole-wheat pecan pancakes.) I recall the board retreat held at Jubilee by Habitat for Humanity International, which at that time included President Jimmy Carter. I have treasured memories of a work team to Egypt and Jordan to build Habitat houses that was organized in 2003 by Don and his wife, Carolyn.

As you read and absorb *Faith Beyond Borders,* you will gain a new vision of the exciting ways a person can serve our Lord and Master. One can see that Don takes seriously Jesus' words: "Father, your kingdom come, your will be done on earth as it is in heaven"; "If you do it to one of the least of these my children, you do it to me"; and especially "Love your enemies."

In 2007, just two years before the end of Millard's life, Don initiated one of the most exciting peacemaking ventures we had ever undertaken—a housing project with the people of North Korea.

Millard was enthusiastic about this challenging and significant project. As this book goes to press, the project's future is still far from certain. And yet, just as when we watched our first efforts at Koinonia Farm and in Mbandaka, Zaire, grow into thousands of housing projects all over the world, we should never be surprised at what God can accomplish through us if we act on our faith, letting love overcome our fears as we work diligently on "heavenly causes."

As you will discover through Don's stories of faith and love in action, there are challenges and opportunities ahead for all of us. Perhaps this book will encourage you to make similar commitments and create inspiring stories of your own.

Linda C. Fuller
Cofounder of Habitat for Humanity International
and the Fuller Center for Housing

Acknowledgments

All books are products of joint efforts by many people, but that is especially true for this one. In a real sense, it is more the story of the stream of courageous refugees and other inspiring people who have touched my life than it is my own story. They lived the story. Often I simply helped to get it onto paper and out to you.

Then there is Joyce Hollyday. As in our earlier joint effort (*With Our Own Eyes,* Herald Press, 1996), this book might never have been completed without her assistance. Time after time I have quickly hammered out narratives about events—often while already preoccupied by the next challenge—and then depended on Joyce to make the accounts more readable. She has done so every time. If you find traces of eloquence here and there you can safely assume that you're seeing Joyce's fingerprints.

I must also mention Ron Kidd, a senior editor at Abingdon Press. I thank God for the day Ron visited Jubilee on other business and we became acquainted. Since then he has provided scores of emails and telephone calls full of good advice and encouragement. He has been extraordinarily patient with a writer who is perpetually trying to do too many things at once!

I am deeply grateful to the other members of the Jubilee Partners community. Why that is true will become obvious as you read this book. Not only have they been the main actors in many of the stories I have told, but they have often taken on extra work while I worked on the manuscript. I cannot imagine a richer environment than the Jubilee community in which to work for peace and justice—and then to write this account.

But most of all, there is my wonderful wife and best friend, Carolyn. As you will see in the following pages, she has played a major role in virtually all the adventures described here. In some cases she has been in the thick of the action. In others she has played a less conspicuous, but essential, supportive role. She is compassionate, courageous, and full of determination to serve God through loving action wherever she may find herself. I am more deeply in love with her each year. This is her story as much as it is mine or anyone else's.

I hope you enjoy it and and that your own faith grows stronger as you read it. We have a lot of work to do in this beautiful, troubled world!

Introduction

Someday, after mastering the winds, the waves, the tides and gravity, we shall harness for God the energies of love, and then, for a second time in the history of the world, [humanity] will have discovered fire.

—Teilhard de Chardin

I surveyed the scene inside our large dining room at Jubilee Partners, the community in northeast Georgia that has been my home for thirty years. Half a dozen long tables were loaded with delicious food from many cuisines around the world—mounds of steaming rice and vegetables, pungent stews, breads in every size and shape, fresh jams and sweet desserts alongside more than 150 pounds of turkey. I can't imagine any restaurant rivaling our menu on Thanksgiving Day 2009! The crowd gathered into two huge concentric circles. We clasped hands and sang a simple song of thanks:

Hands, hands, hands, thank you, God, for hands.
Food, food, food, thank you, God, for food.
Friends, friends, friends, thank you, God, for friends! Amen.

Set up outside was a large white tent containing tables and chairs for 200 guests. After loading up their plates, people streamed into the big tent to feast on the bounty. Dozens of the kids opted to eat in our bright, homemade "carousel" shelter or to scatter around the yard in little groups. Joyful chatter was every-where, as people shared stories about their present activities.

We began our celebration that day on a perfectly beautiful morning on a wooded hillside beside one of our lakes. Sitting on blankets and tarps spread on a soft bed of newly fallen leaves, we looked upward through the tall oaks at a few golden leaves still waving in the soft breeze against the backdrop of a bright blue sky. In a dramatic recitation, Josie Winterfeld quoted from memory the eloquent Nineteenth Psalm as she presented the sermon at our Thanksgiving service. It seemed almost as though the psalmist could have been sitting there at Jubilee on such a day when he wrote these words:

> The heavens tell out the glory of God, the vault of heaven reveals his handiwork. One day speaks to another, night with night shares its knowledge, and this without speech or language or sound of any voice. Their music goes out through all the earth, their words reach to the ends of the world. (NEB)

Even the least poetic among us could grasp the meaning of the psalmist's metaphor of speech and music in the beauty of God's creation all around us. And when Eh Kaw Htoo took his turn in front of the crowd and translated the Scripture and Josie's sermon for the refugees from Myanmar (Burma) who were scattered among us, it was obvious from their murmurs and expressions that they also understood at once.

The truth is that God speaks to us in ways more profound than we can express in mere words or language or sound of any voice. Maybe we at Jubilee were a little more attuned that day to such realities as we marked our thirtieth anniversary year and thought more than usual about how much God has blessed us. Lately those of us who live and work here are simply astonished by the palpable sense of God's loving presence among us.

Even the most skeptical onlooker would have to concede that Thanksgiving was an extraordinary day at Jubilee. About 280 people from sixteen countries worshiped, played games, chatted eagerly with one another, ate together, and, most important of all, affirmed their love for each other and the joy at being together again. They came from every continent, in all the gorgeous colors of humanity, laughing and celebrating: the beautiful work of God's hands.

Families that had first begun to straggle into Jubilee decades earlier, often scarred by war and extreme hunger, by torture camps and prisons, now proudly introduced relatives who had recently followed them to this country, or children who had been born since the parents' time at Jubilee. Old refugee friends warmly hugged one another, as well as Jubilee residents who had taught them their first English lessons. Others, now fluent in English, rejoiced in memories of their first loving reception after years or even decades of rejection and suffering.

At one point in the morning's worship service, the invitation was made to anyone who would like to come to the front and sing. Whatever language was used—Karen, English, Karenni, Spanish, Swahili, Korean—enthusiastic applause always erupted from the congregation.

At the end of the service, Coffee Worth, our oldest resident, was asked to lead us in prayer. She began with her trademark, "Well, here we are, Lord..." Then she proceeded not only to give thanks for the wonderful things that had happened over the past thirty years, but to call for us all to have the faith and the strength to continue the work in the years ahead of us.

Coffee Worth has been around long enough—including twenty-two years as a Presbyterian missionary in South Korea—to know the difference between faith in the power of God's love and shallow optimism. There *will* be great problems ahead, but she demonstrates a joyful confidence in God's presence among us through the worst of them. That is why, just a month before, close to a hundred people joined us in the celebration of her ninetieth birthday. We all like to be near such people.

While we shared our Thanksgiving feast, people wandered a few at a time over to a corner of the yard. There sat a table with a stack of paper, each sheet blank except for the phrase "When I think about my time at Jubilee..." at the top. Many of Jubilee's former residents took the challenge:

"It's great overhere!" wrote one. "When I arrived here, it seems like I go to the mountian. It's quiet, peaceful, and fresh-air. Thank you so much for give me the time to share my feeling overhere!"

Another penned, "I learned to ride a bike, with bruises on both Knees. I remembered learning my first words of English here at Jubilee. I surely missed those wonderful times. Thank-You Jubilee Partners."

A third added, "When I came here, I can know and see clearly about love that Jubilee gives to people who come from another countries.... I appreciate so much about everything Jubilee did for my family."

One young person whose relatives had come through Jubilee from Southeast Asia twenty-five years ago drew a picture of trees under a smiling sun. He wrote, "This is the first time I come to Jubilee because I just come America. I'm from Viet Nam. But I think Jubilee's great place to stand together."

And so do we. And for that we give all the thanks to God, whose "music goes out through all the earth"—including through this little community in northeast Georgia. Catching bits and pieces of that music as we go about our work here, we are also reminded of the beautiful words from Isaiah 43 that tell us not to spend our time brooding about the past, but rather to look around us and discover that God is still doing "a new thing [among you].... Can you not perceive it?" (verse 19, NEB). Our constant prayer is that God will help us perceive what is in store for us to do next.

This book both celebrates what has been and anticipates what is yet to come. It is about walking by faith—not just talking about it, but breaking out of our fear and putting our faith into action.

It's about crossing the borders that exist in our nations, in our communities, and in our hearts.

I have become acutely aware of a phenomenon that operates in so many of us: the constant tendency to dismiss any new idea or experience that challenges our habitual way of looking at the world around us. We tend to be very protective of our familiar understandings, our personal comfort zones. Without realizing it, we can become—as Jesus expressed it in his frustration with even his closest followers—dull of heart and mind.

Jesus offered one particularly fervent outburst after his disciples had personally witnessed a series of dramatic events—from spectacular healings to Jesus' miraculous feeding of a crowd of thousands—and yet continued to be preoccupied with trivia. You can practically see him pacing back and forth as he confronts them: "Have you no inkling yet? Do you still not understand? Are your minds closed? You have eyes: can you not see? You have ears: can you not hear? Have you forgotten?" (Mark 8:17b-19a, NEB).

Let me be clear from the beginning that this book is much more of a confession than a boast. I identify to the core with those disciples. Like them, I have seen God's unmistakable hand in one miracle after another—and then sleepwalked right on along my way, as surely as though I were impaired in sight and hearing, and maybe also suffering from severe memory loss.

The bad news is that so many people all around the world are doing the same, with the result that we are marching toward global catastrophe like lemmings toward the edge of a cliff. It is as though we are determined to destroy life on this planet and simply can't make up our minds whether to do it by nuclear weapons, climate change, biological warfare, or some other means at our disposal.

The good news is that—if we can shake ourselves awake in time, open our eyes and really see—we'll recognize a force for good that is more powerful than all the evils that threaten us. As

Teilhard de Chardin insisted more than half a century ago, we can "harness for God the energies of love."

Greek scholar and Southern Baptist theologian Clarence Jordan founded Koinonia Partners in Americus, Georgia, where my wife, Carolyn, and I lived for eight years before moving to Jubilee Partners. Clarence preached—and demonstrated—what he often referred to as "incarnational evangelism." He argued that we only have the right to bear witness to that which we ourselves put into practice.

In one of his best-known sermons, "The Substance of Faith," Clarence proclaimed, "Faith is not belief in spite of the evidence but a life in scorn of the consequences." He went on to insist, "It is the word become flesh. So long as that word remains a theory to us and is not incarnated by our actions and translated by our deeds into a living experience, it is not faith. It may be theology, but it is not faith. Faith is a combination of both conviction and action."[1]

Audiences listened in rapt attention to Clarence, and not only because he had a way with words. They knew that he and the others at Koinonia were living by that faith. Despite dozens of violent attacks by the Ku Klux Klan and others—from bombings of the community's roadside stand to sprays of gunfire by nightriders—they stood firm in their witness against racism. They continued to live as a "beloved community" of black and white together. Clarence believed that most of us haven't begun to tap the richness of our faith. Referring to Jesus' call to faithfulness in the Sermon on the Mount, he declared, "We are at a banquet table laden with bounties and we are doodlebugging around trying to decide if we want cream of wheat or cold cereal."[2]

Why, Clarence asked, is faith so scarce? His answer was "fear." "Faith and fear, like light and darkness," he preached, "are incompatible. Fear is the polio of the soul which prevents our walking by faith."[3]

Scripture assures us that "perfect love banishes fear" (1 John

4:18, NEB). Most of us have to confess to being far from perfect in our love. But we do have an example of one who showed us the way.

Jesus wasn't just a naïve dreamer who hiked around Galilee mouthing sweet platitudes. He fearlessly confronted a world that was no less filled with danger than is ours. From his earliest childhood, he was surrounded by a bloody struggle between the Roman legions and those of his neighbors who were determined to drive them out by force. Violence was more widespread and constant around Jesus than most of us can imagine. According to historians of the period, many thousands of people were crucified, and tens of thousands more sold into slavery during Jesus' lifetime—all preface to the destruction of Jerusalem and the slaughter of an estimated one million Jews.

Jesus knew about terrorism and military violence as directly as any survivor of the attacks on the Twin Towers in New York City or any soldier on the battlefields of Iraq or Afghanistan today. And yet he commanded, repeatedly and unequivocally, "Put down your swords, and love your enemies." Talk about subversive ideas! This man was dangerous. What if the people gathered around him actually started taking him seriously?

"What if," indeed! What if all the Roman soldiers who came to Palestine found people who loved them, willingly helped them carry their packs, went out looking for chances to give food and water to hungry and thirsty young men far from their homes in Italia? Jesus taught and demonstrated such acts constantly. In the final days before his crucifixion, he could see clearly where the choice of violence was taking Jerusalem. "If only you had known, on this great day, the way that leads to peace," he wept. "But no; it is hidden from your sight" (Luke 19:42, NEB).

One of the best-kept secrets in the world is that such acts of love have proven to be far more powerful throughout history than have all the swords and cruise missiles in which we have trusted instead. Millions of us memorize the beautiful words of Jesus about loving our enemies, or of the apostle Paul and others about overcoming evil with good. Then we absolutely fail to see the obvious gap between what we affirm and what we actually do, especially when we are afraid.

As you will read in the following pages, I have been blessed to see what Teilhard de Chardin called the "energy of love" transform one situation after another in some of the most divided and dangerous places on earth. This book is not a gloomy prediction of inevitable disaster. On the contrary, it is a narrative of hope. It is about the genuine joy and adventure of trying to respond faithfully to our most overwhelming challenges. And it is, most of all, about the exciting realization that the God who created all of it is right here in the thick of things with us.

The prophet Isaiah offered a profound promise to people facing difficult times, to those who grow weary longing for the justice of God and the transformation of the world's broken places. Those who wait and work for healing between peoples and nations, said the prophet, "shall renew their strength." They shall "mount up with wings like eagles" (Isaiah 40:31, NRSV). In far-flung corners of the globe, again and again, I have met people who, by their faith, have overcome their fear, crossed borders both physical and spiritual, and learned to soar. I offer their extraordinary stories here in the hope that they may inspire us to the same.

CHAPTER ONE

Building on Solid Rock

W e decided to build in the middle of Mbandaka. The year was 1974, and the country was Zaire, now known as the Democratic Republic of the Congo. Millard and Linda Fuller and their four children had been there for a year before I arrived. I spent four days coming up the Congo River on a large boat with 200 Zairois passengers, planning to spend a month helping the Fullers launch an ambitious housing project near the place where the river crosses the equator.

The need for housing there was critical. Local government officials had offered Millard his choice of several large pieces of land if he would help solve the shortage. One of those sites was a patch of underbrush with giant termite mounds—some as high as fifteen feet!—that divided the town down the middle. Under orders of the Belgian colonial governor years earlier, it had been left empty as a "sanitation strip" between black Congolese residents and white European settlers living near the river. In the local Lingala language, that strip of land was known as Bokotola: "One who does not like others."

The morning after I arrived in Mbandaka, Millard and I looked over the various available parcels of land. We quickly agreed that it was time to claim Bokotola for the people. The mayor of Mbandaka supplied us with a crew of thirty to fifty men each day.

We worked hard from dawn until dusk, clearing lines of sight, laying out roads and a playground, and driving corner stakes. Sometimes I scrambled up to the top of a termite mound with my surveying instrument and worked over the tops of the small trees. One very busy and exhausting month later, I had finished the survey work and drawn the plans for the first few houses. Eventually, more than a hundred would fill the site.

Little did I suspect, as we worked under the hot sun in the heart of Africa, that we were laying out what would become the first of thousands of Habitat for Humanity projects around the world. Nor could I foresee that two years later, when eighty families were living in their new homes, the Congolese would rename Bokotola. It is now called Losanganya: "Reconciler, everyone together."

I had first encountered Millard Fuller in 1970 at Koinonia Partners, where my wife, Carolyn, and I arrived that summer as volunteers. Carolyn and I had met a few years earlier in Waco, Texas, where she was finishing a master's degree at Baylor University and teaching. When I met her, I had recently returned from two years in Malaysia, serving as one of the earliest Peace Corps volunteers as the conflict in Vietnam was expanding just north of us.

Like me, Carolyn was eager to follow the example of Jesus and serve other people, and she has been a wonderful partner in such work ever since. After marrying, we headed for South Korea, where I served as director of a hundred Peace Corps volunteers along the demilitarized zone during an especially tense period between North and South Korea. In Asia, I had the opportunity to make close friends not only with other Christians but also with Muslims, Buddhists, Hindus, and people of other religions.

Interspersed with these activities were periods when I worked as a mechanical engineer in my father's factory in Texas. But I couldn't shake the feeling that I should find a way to deal more directly with the tensions between people, across racial as well as national boundaries. I particularly wanted to try to work effectively for peace in a world that was threatening to destroy itself through an escalating nuclear arms race.

I loved my father and hated to disappoint him, but Carolyn and I finally decided to leave his business and move to Koinonia, where our volunteer stint stretched into eight of the richest and most intense years of our lives. I arrived at the community with a brand-new graduate degree in anthropology. But I was drawn by the way these Koinonia people were doing things instead of just talking and writing about them.

Clarence Jordan had died just a few months earlier, and the overt violence against the community for its policies of racial equality had all but ended. But racism certainly had not. Slavery had long since been replaced by sharecropping and similarly exploitative arrangements throughout the South, leaving many African American families in dire poverty. Tumbledown shacks lined the back roads surrounding Koinonia.

In 1968, Clarence and Millard had launched the Fund for Humanity, soliciting donations for a revolving account that was used to finance the construction of modest homes. The two of them had great gifts that complemented each other, with Clarence providing a deep understanding of the Gospels, while Millard brought business experience and boundless energy. Clarence had zealously marked off lots for forty houses on the north end of Koinonia's property, but he died of a heart attack six weeks before the first house was completed. Though they had only a few months together as a team before Clarence's death, during that short time Clarence and Millard launched Koinonia into a new orbit.

The housing project continued at full speed under Millard's direction. Early in 1972, he came striding across the yard toward me. "Don, I want you to take charge of Koinonia's housing program," he announced.

"Millard," I protested, "I can't do that. I never built a house in my life! I'm a mechanical engineer, not a building contractor."

"No problem. You're the closest thing we've got to a contractor. I'm sure you'll learn fast."

And sure enough, I did. Half a dozen block houses had already been built at Koinonia by locally hired builders, and we were beginning to attract a stream of hearty young volunteers who were eager to help. Several of them had grown up on Mennonite farms in Pennsylvania, and they were used to hard work. From time to time a professional builder would visit Koinonia for a week or two, and we would surround him to learn whatever we could. We eventually developed into a construction team that produced a solid new house every month.

A year after I took over as supervisor of construction, in January 1973, Millard and Linda and their four children moved to Zaire. They saw up close that the terrible injustices we were observing in southwest Georgia could be found on the other side of the world as well. Millard invited me to come and help him in Mbandaka, where we worked and watched a site of enmity be transformed into a community of reconciliation by love put into action. "Bokotola" became "Losanganya."

A few months later, on July 2, 1974, I wrote to Millard from Koinonia about a vision that was taking shape in my mind, welcoming his comments. "My primary interest," I wrote, "is in setting up a center which could train and reorient capable young (or otherwise) people toward careers—brief or lifelong—of service to the Third World. I want to do that in a setting inspired by Christian values." I closed by asking whether he and Linda might be interested in joining Carolyn and me in such a venture.

Millard's reply, which was dated two weeks later, was full of his characteristic enthusiasm. He outlined what he was also thinking of as a "worldwide poverty housing center," explaining that he envisioned it as a "base for sharing ideas and spiritual truths." He liked the idea of training people for service, and he also imagined a speaking ministry. "Of course," he wrote, "we'll need to correspond a lot on many details, but Linda and I are top of the list interested."

The Fullers returned to Koinonia, where I was then serving as director, in the spring of 1976. In September of that year, twenty-seven of us gathered in what had once been one of Koinonia's chicken houses. Mompongo Mo Imana, or "Sam," as he was known to us, came all the way from Zaire to participate. He was proving to be a dynamic leader as he was carrying forward our work in the village of Ntondo. For two days we prayed and brainstormed about how the amazingly successful projects in Zaire might be replicated. That meeting marked the birth of Habitat for Humanity International.

During those same days, a neighbor just seven miles across the peanut fields from us was entering the final phase of his bid to become president of the United States. Jimmy Carter had been propelled into electoral politics by one of the same forces that were giving birth to Habitat for Humanity: a desire to overcome the evils of racism with compassionate work for justice. In his first entry into politics, as a member of the Sumter County Board of Education, Carter had been so disturbed by the rampant racism of some of the other officials and so determined to do something about it that he decided to run for office at the state level. After serving in the state senate and as governor of Georgia, he had set his sights on the White House. All of us would have been amazed if we had been able to see then the decades ahead of us, full of rich friendships and joint adventures all over the world.

The following spring we had the official founding meeting of the Habitat for Humanity board of directors at the Stony Point Conference Center, an hour up the Hudson River from New York City. Millard was in constant motion, speaking at dozens of churches and conferences. All of us who were involved in Habitat leadership in those early days were enthusiastic about the way the idea was spreading from one community to another. But not in our wildest dreams would we have believed that we had started something that thirty years later would provide housing in a hundred countries for more than a million people.

What we did know was that we were finding people everywhere we went who were suffering from lack of decent shelter. And we consistently felt deep affection and respect develop between us as we worked beside them to solve the problem. Something much more important than house construction was happening at every work site.

We knew that we needed to *act* on our faith, to live by the words of Jesus and not just speak about them. During this time, I thought often of a discussion that a group of us at Koinonia had one day about a serious problem of racial discrimination in the local schools. One of the more cautious people in the circle kept insisting that we needed to be very patient, to let the offenders think about the consequences of their racist position. I could see that Tom Boone, a member of our board of directors, was not happy with that suggestion.

"I'm sorry, but I disagree," Tom said emphatically. "People act their way into new ways of thinking far more often than they think their way into new ways of acting!" I couldn't help smiling. Not only did I agree with him, but it struck me as entirely appropriate that such a statement should come from a man whose uncle (a few generations back, of course) was Daniel Boone—another man who knew something about taking action, about moving out of comfort zones into new territory.

I have come to regard Tom's comment as one of the most profound insights I have ever encountered. *Thinking* is essential, of course. But it is almost always when we reach the point of taking thoughtful *action* that we truly grow in our understanding.

I began to see that response as a succinct paraphrase of Jesus' concluding thought in the Sermon on the Mount. Jesus said quite plainly that those who hear his words and act on them are like a wise man who builds his house on solid rock. But those who do not act are like the foolish man who builds his house on sand, which is easily beaten down by rain and floods and wind (Matthew 7:24-27). I wanted, both literally and figuratively, to be a wise homebuilder, choosing a solid foundation.

Concurrent with these exciting first months of Habitat's existence, a group of about a dozen Koinonia people began to meet regularly to explore some of the other ideas Millard and I had raised in our correspondence. We were particularly interested in helping to establish a new community. We envisioned a community emphasizing peace and justice issues with an international service component.

By 1978 these meetings had progressed to a decision by three families to serve as the pioneers in this new community. Having made the proposal, Carolyn and I became the first to commit ourselves to help start the venture. We were soon joined by Ed and Mary Ruth Weir, and a few days later by Ryan and Karen Karis. All of us agreed that the beautiful passage Jesus had chosen to read in Nazareth, from Isaiah 61, described the vision that was developing among us:

> The spirit of the Lord is upon me because he has anointed me; he has sent me to announce good news to the poor, to proclaim release for prisoners and recovery of sight for the blind; to let the broken victims go free, to proclaim the year of the Lord's favour. (Luke 4:18-19, NEB)

The "year of the Lord's favor" referred to the Jubilee year. According to Leviticus 25, every fifty years throughout the history of the Israelites, prisoners were to be set free, debts were to be forgiven, land was to be returned to its original owners, and the poor were to be given a share of the resources. Jubilee was a year marked by justice and mercy—themes that throbbed at the center of God's good news, from the Old Testament prophets to Jesus.

We decided easily to name our new community Jubilee Partners. But even after dozens of meetings in our living rooms at

Koinonia, our mission was still not clear to us. In fact, it was not even clear where the community should be located. We all shared the sense that we were being called to serve God in a particular way, but the details were very, very murky.

Weekend after weekend we all crowded into our old Dodge van, which we had named "Osmosis"—six adults, six children, and all our camping gear—and set out on a search. On the twelfth trip we finally found it: 260 acres of rolling meadows and forest-land about a hundred miles east of Atlanta, at the edge of the small town of Comer, Georgia. We scraped together just enough money for the down payment, and our friends at Koinonia helped us get a loan from the bank to make the purchase.

In April 1979, Ryan and Karen moved to the property and began their many months of living in a borrowed pop-up camper. The other two families joined them after our children finished the school year. All of us considered camping to be a pleasant vacation activity, and we looked forward to this pioneering phase at Jubilee as more of the same.

Our children, Tony and Robyn, were ten and six at the time, still small enough that the whole Mosley family could just barely squeeze into our two-person backpacking tent. We slept with three sleeping bags pressed side by side, with little Robyn crowded in at our feet. We were awakened on one of our first mornings by a noise that began as a faint rumbling far away and soon escalated into a thundering roar. The ground shook, and one of the children screamed, "Daddy, what's happening?"

Moments later, I was standing in cold, wet grass, waving my arms and shouting as a hundred cows and their calves bolted past. One small calf tripped over our tent rope as the others charged down the hill toward the ponds. "Looks like we survived another stampede," Ryan announced, standing outside his yellow tent. Ed was untangling himself from a clothesline that had fallen, with its row of wet swimsuits and towels, into the mud. Putting up the electric fence got moved that day to the top of our work list.

We knew we were taking on some big challenges, of course, and tackling a lot of unknowns. But it wasn't until we had made the leap that the full reality hit us. Our new site was beautiful, but we had an enormous amount of work to do to get the first houses built, the water and septic systems in place, an entrance road laid—the list suddenly seemed endless. We estimated that it would cost $131,000 and take between twenty and thirty thousand hours of labor to complete.

We kept to a grueling routine of working from early morning until nearly dark. The Georgia sun beat down on us as we dug, hammered, and painted, with only occasional breaks to swim in the ponds. Just before dark each day, we took turns by families bathing in a secluded section of the creek. Careful coordination was required for everyone to finish before the mosquitoes came out. After a few weeks, we all had to admit that bathing in the creek just wasn't the same as a hot shower. As the weeks passed, the novelty of being pioneers wore thin.

Furthermore, we had left Koinonia with a grand total of $26,000 in our joint bank account. We had no jobs and no mailing list. Our friends at Koinonia and Habitat for Humanity had granted us permission back in the spring to send out a notice to their supporters, but we didn't even know what we might say if and when we managed to mail out our first Jubilee newsletter. And we had only a few weeks before the first freezing weather would hit.

It was precisely because of our experience of relative insecurity that we began to pay more attention to the stories we heard on our little battery-powered radio about the suffering of the Vietnamese "boat people." They were refugees who were desperately trying to escape chaos and persecution in their war-torn country. Had we heard the same reports a year or two earlier, we would have felt momentary sympathy for them at most. Now, even though our situation was far more tolerable and safe than theirs, we were beginning to empathize with them. We were uprooted and adrift just enough to have a sense of what they must be feeling.

The cover story of *Newsweek* on July 2, 1979, was titled "Agony of the Boat People." The photograph on the front showed an open boat crowded with refugees, most of them children. In the middle of the crowd sat a woman with a look of fatigue and despair. A crying child sat in her lap, pulling at her.

The article inside reported that three-quarters of a million people had streamed out of Southeast Asia in the previous four years. Of the many who had fled in crowded, leaky boats, up to half had died at sea. I found it especially painful to know that our own nation's violence in the Vietnam War—napalm and bombing raids, defoliation of crops with Agent Orange, and scorched-earth policies toward rural villages—had been a major cause of their dislocation and suffering. By the time I read the story through a second time, I was sure that we had found our work—or been found by it.

A plan quickly began to take shape. Now, at long last, we saw what we were being called to do. We began to dream of a place of hospitality for refugees, where we would offer lessons in basic English and cultural orientation and arrange sponsors for the next phase of their lives. We set out to build a Welcome Center for these refugees, hoping to share community with them and ease some of their suffering.

Our mission seemed confirmed when I went to a national conference and heard a preacher use the text from Isaiah 54:2-3: "Enlarge the limits of your home, spread wide the curtains of your tent; let out its ropes to the full and drive the pegs home" (NEB). We had no idea at the beginning just how far we would be asked to stretch, or how much blessing would come to us in the stretching.

Even greater confirmation came when we sent out our first newsletter, describing our dream and requesting contributions, non-interest loans, and volunteer labor. We had no idea if people would respond, but we tried to trust that all was in God's hands.

The first response came a few days later. It was from Willie Mae Champion, a longtime employee and neighbor of Koinonia, who had worked closely with Clarence Jordan, and then with me, on many projects.

Willie Mae was writing to tell us how much she loved us, assuring us that she would be praying for the success of our work. Having grown up in a poor sharecropper's shack had given her understanding into the plight of refugees. She had no funds to contribute to our work, but her letter was worth far more to me than any amount of money.

The next day brought half a dozen more responses. The day after that, the dam broke. We were astonished as letters poured in almost faster than we could open or respond to them. In the evenings we sat around our dining room table and took turns reading them aloud, sometimes laughing, often with tears in our eyes. We began to realize that we would have hundreds of true partners in this work.

One car after another began to arrive with helpers, offering anywhere from a few hours to a month of free labor. Our property began to resemble a campground as tents, trailers, and RVs filled up the empty spaces. To our amazement, people seemed always to show up with the right skills just when we needed them.

Meanwhile, we did our best to build solid personal friendships with our neighbors. Predictably, there was some anxiety about a group of "outsiders" coming into a small Georgia town and establishing a center for refugees from all over the globe. We were bringing something very new to Comer. A reporter from the regional newspaper was assigned to write an "exposé" about the Jubilee "commune." Our neighbors soon learned that there was nothing to expose, and our appreciation for their warmth and generosity has only deepened over the years.

We worked at absolute maximum speed to get our Welcome Center ready. In September 1980, I got the call from New York that we had been waiting for. Several members of Jubilee were taking a break in our large community kitchen. At the first lull in the conversation, I announced as casually as I could that our first fourteen refugees would be arriving at the Atlanta airport the following morning.

"Tomorrow morning! But we're still painting their cabin. Their bunks aren't finished. . ." Everyone seemed to be talking at once, excited that our long wait was over but also nervous now that the moment had arrived. Our first guests were going to be Cuban "boat people" rather than Vietnamese, sponsored by the United Methodist Committee on Relief and Church World Service.

That spring, a trickle of Cubans had successfully crossed the eighty miles of open sea to Florida. But the trickle quickly grew to a torrent, as Cuban leader Fidel Castro opened prisons and released the inmates to come, along with the others, to the United States. By midsummer more than 100,000 newly arrived Cubans were in Florida, and the refugee resettlement officials with whom we had been working in preparation for receiving Southeast Asians pleaded with us to take Cubans first.

I made a visit to the Immigration and Naturalization Services detention center just outside Miami and interviewed a long line of men who had come to Florida and been picked up by the U.S. Coast Guard. They were desperate to leave the stockade where they were imprisoned behind a ten-foot, chain-link fence topped with coils of barbed concertina wire. With no trees and little grass in the compound, they were on hot sand in blazing sun, crowded into a few large tents and some rusty World War II airplane hangars.

The first man I interviewed was named Rodolfo Portillo. His wife had become ill in Havana and was not responding to the medicine at the government clinic. He could not afford the more expensive treatment she needed. Against her pleas that he not leave her and their children, he got on a crowded fishing boat and headed to the United States to try to earn money to save his wife's life.

In Florida the Coast Guard arrested him almost immediately. For three months he begged to be released from the detention center to help his family. "Yesterday I received word that I am too late," he told me, his eyes filling with tears. "My wife has died." He was desperate to get out and help his children.

I heard many similarly compelling stories and wished that we could bring all the men to Jubilee. I chose fourteen of them, and they became the first of thousands from around the world to come through our Welcome Center. After fifteen months of hard work, with more than a hundred volunteers, we finished the refugee cabins and other basic essentials with just hours to spare. Our first guests came straggling off the plane at the Atlanta airport, with Rodolfo leading the way, smiling broadly. Two hours later we rounded the curve at the Jubilee parking lot and were met by a cheering crowd with a big, handwritten sign: *"Bienvenidos—* Welcome."

We hosts discovered that we had a few things to learn. We thought, for example, that it would be great for the refugees to have a free night in the nearby city of Athens. We blithely dropped them off at a corner and asked them to meet us back there in two hours. They pulled out all the stops, drinking, pinching women, and arguing with local men who had no idea what they were saying. And, of course, they were not all waiting at the corner at the appointed time. We spent hours hunting for some of them. One was delivered to Jubilee the next morning by the Athens police.

But the following evening they were the picture of contrition. And our initial anxiety eventually gave way to strong ties of friendship and affection. The men worked hard to learn English, and we worked hard to find sponsors for them. We were so successful that Church World Service soon asked us to take twenty-four more.

Two dozen gregarious, swashbuckling Cuban men were enough to send shock waves through our little Georgia town. One evening in mid-December, a Jubilee volunteer ran into the community house, shouting, "Luis just tried to slug Mayor Yarborough and Marlin Carithers while they were on police duty!"

Luis was a friendly, easygoing man who had been in prison in Cuba for a petty crime. He had ridden his bike that night to a store in Comer. On his way back to Jubilee, he found himself being followed by a car with a flashing blue light.

"I didn't know what that light meant," he told us later, "so I tried to beat them back to Jubilee. I thought it was some hoodlums following me."

The "hoodlums" were our part-time police force. They were concerned that Luis was riding without any lights and had tried to stop him. When he fell off his bike, they got out to talk with him, but Luis didn't know English. Cliff Yarborough reached out to reassure him, and Luis thought he was going to strike him, so he took a swing at Comer's mayor. Fortunately, he missed him.

The next day Luis was retelling the story to his friends, marveling that he had not been put in jail. The refugees became quiet when they spied the Comer police car coming down the winding Jubilee road. Cliff and Marlin got out of the car, announcing, "Hello, fellows, we've got a little Christmas present for you." While Luis and his friends looked on in utter astonishment, the two men opened the back of the car and took out two bushels of fresh fruit for the refugees. We were witnesses that day to a rare and beautiful act of genuine Christian peacemaking by two of our neighbors. I was ready to nominate Mayor Cliff Yarborough for the Nobel Peace Prize.

We watched with great satisfaction as all our Cuban guests learned English and moved on to cities with sponsoring churches and families, according to our hopes and plans. All, that is, except the brothers Pablo and Ramon. Pablo had a weakness for alcohol, and Ramon was severely limited intellectually. They were sweet and very lovable, but utterly unable to learn English. Our most common prayer at lunch became, "And, Lord, please help us find a sponsor for Pablo and Ramon."

Then one afternoon I got a tip about a rancher near Austin, Texas, who was looking for two men to take care of his breed bulls. I was honest in our phone call about the brothers' limitations. But occasional drunkenness, poor language ability, and a lack of mechanical skills weren't viewed as drawbacks by this rancher.

At Jubilee we had had a lot of celebrations, but never was there greater exuberance than that day. Even the most skeptical among us became believers in the power of prayer. A year later, I had an opportunity to visit Pablo and Ramon on the Texas ranch and found them, and the rancher, happy and thrilled with the arrangement.

As the years have passed, we have hosted more than 3,000 refugees from dozens of countries all over the globe. About half of our staff of approximately two dozen people is made up of year-round residents ("resident partners"). The other half are volunteers who come for several months at a time to help us in all aspects of Jubilee's work. Almost a thousand outstanding people have participated in our volunteer program. In addition, we host a constant stream of visitors, between one and two thousand each year.

In bold print across the first copy of the Jubilee Partners newsletter, we placed this quote from Hebrews 11:1, in Clarence Jordan's Cottonpatch version: "Now faith is the turning of dreams into deeds; it is betting your life on the unseen realities." More than we could ever have foreseen, the river of battered survivors of some of the world's greatest tragedies that has flowed through our lives has enriched us and helped us understand and love people from every corner of the earth. We are reminded every day that in our home, as well as in our hearts, there is always more room. And, as on that overgrown strip of land that divided Mbandaka, Zaire, down the middle more than three decades ago, separation and suspicion can be transformed into "everyone together."

CHAPTER TWO

But I Say Unto You. . .

The sixteen-year-old from Bosnia had tears in her eyes. She listened raptly, focusing on words in a language that was new to her, as George White told us his story. George's wife had been killed in southern Alabama, and even though the gunman had also wounded him, a local court convicted George of the murder. He spent several agonizing years in prison, unfairly accused and mourning his wife, before he was able to prove his innocence. During those years his teenage children stood by him, helping him to overcome the hatred he felt toward the killer and all who had been part of the gross miscarriage of justice that had almost cost him his life along with his wife's.

George came to Jubilee as part of a group touring around the country called Murder Victims' Families for Reconciliation. All its members had lost a loved one to violence. And all had made the painful journey through grief to forgiveness, realizing that their feelings of anger and vengeance toward those who had robbed them of beloved family members were an obstacle to their own healing.

The year was 1994, and the majority of refugees with us then were from Bosnia-Herzegovina, a tiny nation that was caught up in bloody ethnic strife. Two years earlier, I had organized a delegation of two Muslims, a Jew, and seven Christians to the neighboring country of Croatia. Many Croatian Roman Catholics had joined with the Orthodox Christians of Serbia in a campaign of terror against Bosnian Muslims.

Through many hours of interviewing, we learned in great detail about Europe's worst atrocity since World War II. We heard stories of concentration camps and mass executions. We learned of women and girls escaping from "rape camps," some several months pregnant, others near insanity as a result of their relentless torture, and a few so ill they were near death. We heard things that I wanted to believe were not possible.

In the center of the town of Karlovac, a thousand men just released from the horrendous Serbian prison camp at Omarska were arriving at a three-story barracks. Hundreds of people were gathered in front of the building, many of them wives frantically searching for their husbands. Shouts of joy mingled with sobs of sorrow as some were reunited and others learned of loved ones who had died in the camp.

Although I didn't know it at the time, among the newly released prisoners that day were three men who would be among the first Bosnian refugees to arrive at Jubilee six months later. Many of those who eventually came to us expressed a similar sentiment: "I don't understand what happened. For years we were neighbors, often best friends, without any regard for ethnic backgrounds. Then, this demonic force called 'ethnic cleansing' broke out among us. And now we are killing each other on sight."

Altogether, about 400 Bosnians came as our refugee guests. We helped hundreds more reunite with their families. We did our best to demonstrate to these mostly Muslim brothers and sisters a version of Christianity that all too few of them had ever experienced. Working, playing, and celebrating with them enriched and expanded our own faith.

The evening of George White's visit, after he finished relating his story, I leaned over to the Bosnian teenager, who was still learning English, and asked, "Could you understand?"

"Yes," she replied. "I understand—but I don't understand. A man kill your wife, and you forgive that man? I don't understand how it is possible!" She stood up, her eyes brimming with tears. "I hope," she began haltingly, "I hope I can forgive the Serbs like that in ten years."

I called George over and shared with him what she had said. He looked into her eyes, put his hands gently on her shoulders, and said, "Honey, you have to try. It's the only way to heal from this mess."

Of all the challenging words of Jesus, I believe the most difficult are these from his Sermon on the Mount: "You have heard that it was said, 'You shall love your neighbor and hate your enemy.' But I say to you, Love your enemies and pray for those who persecute you" (Matthew 5:43-44, NRSV). We started Jubilee Partners with a mission to offer hospitality to refugees, but over the years we have learned that we are also called in very concrete ways to love our enemies, particularly people labeled so by our government. By the time that Bosnian teenager came to Jubilee, we had seen that difficult challenge raised in dozens of situations among the stream of refugees that came from all over the world.

As the last of the Cubans prepared to leave Jubilee, we found ourselves grieving to see them go. Many of them left weeping. One said as we departed for the airport, "I have not had a family like this for many years." But we did not have time to linger long on the sadness. Southeast Asians were already knocking on our door.

In early 1981 we received word that six Laotian and Hmong families were on their way. The remaining Cubans pitched in to help us get ready for them, adding their labor to the construction of our new school. At the Atlanta airport, the new refugees were exhausted after thirty-six hours of travel, and they still had two more hours in the car to Jubilee, but they were smiling and gracious.

Heavy rain had both delayed their flight and slowed down our road trip. The impatient Cubans back at Jubilee decided that a little beer would help pass the time while they waited. At midnight, we finally turned the last corner and pulled up at the Welcome Center. Six exuberant—and slightly drunk—Cubans came spilling out the front door, shouting "Welcome!" at the startled Laotians.

The Cubans all but carried our new guests into their homes. The yard was covered in thick mud. Each time a smiling Laotian entered a cabin, shoes were carefully left at the front door. Each time a smiling Cuban followed, a new trail of mud was tracked across the floor.

In the ensuing days, we marveled at the way the goodwill of each group overcame the barriers of our three contrasting cultures. The children were best at this, and the Laotian boys and girls spent hours each day playing with their new, big Cuban friends. When the time came for the last Cubans to depart, there were Laotian as well as North American tears.

We soon lost track of the number of trips we made to the Atlanta airport to pick up families arriving from Southeast Asia. Thirty Laotians, a hundred Cambodians, and 313 Vietnamese passed through Jubilee. Most of them arrived from the other side of the world without any exposure to such amenities as telephones and flush toilets, but they calmly followed us up and down escalators, along moving sidewalks, and through underground trains that moved from one airport concourse to another guided by computers rather than human drivers.

When one Laotian family discovered the fat field mice in the Jubilee forest, the refugees were thrilled, having worried that they would never get to enjoy this favorite delicacy in the United States. Soon little shovel holes appeared around the bases of the trees, signs of enthusiastic hunters. One day excitement swept the Welcome Center as word spread of a "very big mouse" that had fallen into an empty trash barrel. Someone went to the barrel and looked into the face of an angry, hissing opossum.

We provided the refugees with donated clothing and a modest allowance for food and other necessities. From time to time they prepared elaborate feasts for us. They worked for hours cooking delicious egg rolls, huge mounds of steamed and fried rice, and many special dishes from their respective traditions. We were moved to know that they had paid for the food by limiting purchases for their own families. Those evenings always ended with carefully prepared and rehearsed speeches in broken English, expressions of appreciation and gratitude that came from the heart.

I will never forget a moment in an informal worship service when we were each asked to draw something for which we were thankful. It was October, so I quickly drew a leaf to illustrate my appreciation for the colorful foliage in the Jubilee woods. The woman across from me had made a crude drawing of one man shooting another and a woman with two children running away. "When we try escape from Laos to Thailand, a soldier catch us," she explained as tears ran down her face. "He say he will kill all of us. My husband say, 'No! Kill me and let wife and children go.' The soldier kill my husband and let us run away. I thank God for my good husband."

Every one of the hundred Cambodians who came through Jubilee in less than a year had lost relatives in the mass slaughter and starvation that visited that country when the brutal Khmer Rouge turned it into a vast "killing field." Hunger and hard labor dominated the lives of the Uong family for four years after they were pushed out of Phnom Penh. Even two-year-old Srey was forced to spend several hours every day gathering dung in a bucket for fertilizer.

Srey's father had been shot to death. Her mother, about to give birth and unable to travel with the rest of the extended family, had to be left behind and was never heard from again. Srey's grandmother, 47-year-old widow Soum Sirk, was the intrepid matriarch of the large family.

When life became intolerable, the family decided to escape to Thailand. They split into four groups to try to avoid being detected on their dangerous and arduous three-day journey to the border. They walked at night through jungles and rice paddies, passing craters made by U.S. bombs. They hid during the day in brush, always fearing that some of them would not survive to be reunited at a Red Cross camp across the border. What an incredibly joyful moment when the last group appeared. Seventeen-year-old Phamaret rode into the camp on a bicycle with his younger sister Pechmony on the back and little Srey bouncing in the basket on the front!

During the two years that the Uong family waited for an overseas sponsor, they learned English and trade skills. Before their arrival at Jubilee, we received a letter from them: "We do hope that you are very kind and always have a high willing to save the suffering people of all nations. We have a great aim to go and live quietly in your beautiful country." After apologies for their "poor English," they closed with a promise: "We will try to learn more that will make us having the possibility to speak and be easy to live with."

If only all the world were so easy to live with!

The children learned English at an amazing rate and chattered incessantly. At Christmas, with shining eyes and broad smiles, they received from Ryan Karis, Karen Karis, and Robbie Buller stockings filled with fruit, candy, and small gifts. In their short lives, spent mostly in overcrowded refugee camps, the children had enjoyed precious little of such delights. But they followed the Jubilee folks back to their homes, emptied their stockings, and insisted on sharing the contents with the givers.

A year later, our attention was turned to another part of the world that was suffering as a result of the policies of our own nation. In November 1982, Eric Drewry and I met eight Guatemalans at their hiding place in Brownsville, Texas. "It has been a very hard trip, señor," said one. "The coyotes [refugee smugglers] took all of our money and abandoned us."

A bloody struggle was taking place in Guatemala. It was a story we would hear again and again in the years to come—of helpless peasants caught between the brutality of the Central American military forces on one side and local guerilla fighters on the other. These young men had been the objects of recruitment attempts from both sides. They told of bombed villages and massacres of entire families.

In Guatemala and El Salvador, U.S.-based fruit and mining companies had joined forces with elite landholding minorities, consigning the landless masses to desperate poverty. Attempts at land reform and other justice campaigns were met with unspeakable brutality, carried out by death squads and by soldiers supported by U.S. tax dollars. Among the most prominent victims in El Salvador were four U.S. churchwomen, six Jesuit priests, and San Salvador's archbishop Oscar Romero.

Guatemalans and Salvadorans were flooding across the Texas border, pleading for refuge. Instead of being offered protection, they were rounded up and crowded into jails and concentration camps, then herded in groups through rapid "hearings" before Immigration and Naturalization Service judges. At the rate of about a thousand a month, they were being deported back into the hands of the very governments they had fled, which meant, for many, almost certain death. Reagan administration policy toward Central Americans was resulting in a miscarriage of justice on a massive scale.

We knew we had to do something. At Jubilee our work to that point had been with the full cooperation of the U.S. government. Now we realized we would have to take actions that would be controversial at best and perhaps even illegal. "What would Jesus do?" became the question underlying all others. What would we do if we found ourselves having to choose between cooperation with U.S. policy and faithfulness to God? After several long meetings and a lot of prayer, we decided we must help the refugees, whatever the risk.

Several congregations across the United States had already

launched the Sanctuary Movement, declaring their churches places of refuge for those labeled "illegal aliens" by our government. Arrests of some for their conspiracy of compassion were just around the corner. Friends in Canada were reviving the idea of the Underground Railroad, which had carried fugitive slaves to their country a century before. They established an "Overground Railroad" network to usher Central American refugees to safety.

Our contribution was a program called the *Año de Jubileo*— "Year of Jubilee." We purchased a bus and made more than sixty trips to the Rio Grande Valley in south Texas, bringing those refugees who were in the greatest danger of persecution or death if they were forced to return to their own countries. We learned that we could apply for political asylum for each of them and gain them six months of legal residence in the United States. That was more than enough time to arrange interviews for them at Jubilee with the Canadian Consulate, give them a few months of English classes and cultural orientation, and then carry them to Canada and a new life as legal refugees there.

For eight years we hosted a steady stream of refugees from the bloody civil wars of Central America, more than 1,300 in all. Most had faced obstacles and anguish of a sort that we could barely comprehend. We heard endless accounts of dangerous river crossings and nights spent hiding from the sweep of Border Patrol searchlights, crawling through snake-infested fields, and fighting off the torment of mosquitoes.

One young woman had set out for the United States with her infant daughter. She was caught in Mexico, jailed for months, and raped repeatedly by her guards. When she was released, she waded across the Rio Grande carrying her small daughter above her head. She gave birth soon afterward to the daughter of one of her rapists. Nuns hid the little family for several months until our bus picked them up. When the young mother related her story at Jubilee, baby Melisa sat in her lap smiling and chortling, blissfully oblivious of the suffering her mother had endured to bring her and her older sister to safety.

Inspired by the story of a young Guatemalan named Roberto and by the biblical story of Paul and Silas being sprung from jail by an earthquake (Acts 16:25-26), we established the "Paul and Silas Revolving Bail Fund." That effort raised bond money for the release of a steady stream of refugees from the *Corralón,* or "Big Corral," as the refugees called the detention center on the Texas border. Roberto's crime was that, as a student in Guatemala, he had been involved in literacy work, distribution of food and medicine, and running an agricultural cooperative. Members of a death squad seized him, tortured and beat him, and left him for dead in Guatemala City's huge garbage dump.

Thousands of Guatemala's poorest people, many of them women and children, live and work at the dump, with hundreds of buzzards circling overhead and emaciated dogs watching for a chance to dart in for food. They live in tiny shacks that hang precariously on the brink of the garbage canyon. The shacks are sometimes washed loose by heavy rains or shaken by earthquakes, and plummet into the abyss with their occupants, who literally become part of the slowly moving, filthy glacier of garbage. The dump has always been a popular place for death squads to dispose of bodies.

Roberto, who survived the death squads, regained consciousness in a garbage worker's shack. Almost three months later, he waded across the Rio Grande into Texas. Within twenty-four hours, the Border Patrol had seized him and begun deportation hearings, despite Roberto's frantic protests that deportation would mean certain death for him.

We began raising money for Roberto and for other desperate refugees like him. In the process, we created a massive "prison break" for hundreds of people by a method that was entirely legal. Our friends lent us more than $100,000 with which we established a revolving bail fund. From this "Paul and Silas Revolving Bail Fund," we paid the bail for many refugee prisoners and brought them to Jubilee. The Canadian officials interviewed them, approved their refugee status, and gave us permission to bus them on up to Canada. As soon as the "escapees" crossed into Canada, U.S. authorities had to repay the bond money to us. We promptly used it to free the next candidate in line.

Pedro, a sad young man of sixteen who missed his mother terribly, had paid a heavy price for his belief in nonviolence. He was traveling all alone and often sat under a tree at Jubilee strumming his guitar and singing softly. "My mother always read the Bible and prayed with us every night," he told me. "She loved the Sermon on the Mount. She read to us many times where Jesus taught us that we should love our neighbors—even our enemies."

Both Pedro and his younger brother had been drafted into the Salvadoran army. They were sent into the mountains to kill guerillas, having been told that they themselves would be killed if they didn't follow orders. One day Pedro was leading a patrol of boys, all younger than he, and they came upon a guerilla. "I aimed my rifle at him and tried to squeeze the trigger, but just then I thought about my mother reading to us that we should love our enemies. I could not shoot."

Pedro lowered his rifle and motioned to the others to go back. "Then the guerilla heard us," he continued. "He whirled around and started shooting at us. I think my brother was the first to die." Pedro was shot in the foot, but he managed to escape. Crushed by the death of his brother and the others, he decided to kill himself with a hand grenade, but one of his officers intervened and persuaded him not to do it.

Pedro was allowed to leave the army, but he started receiving death threats. One note warned that if he didn't leave El Salvador, he would be killed within twenty-four hours. He tearfully tore himself away from his mother and left for the United States. "I wish I could be home with her again," he said softly as he picked up his guitar again and began strumming. I was humbled by the way he had been true at such a young age to the same teachings of Jesus that I had embraced without such cost.

Our belief in "love for enemies" was tested in a very different way by another young man. Robbie Buller was interviewing the young man when he explained that in El Salvador, every Saturday night he received a list of individuals on whose doors he and his comrades were supposed to knock. "If they let us in, we were simply to take them away and turn them over to our superiors. But if they would not let us in, we were to break in. If we found them, we were to execute them." It became very obvious that the man had been a member of a death squad.

After telling his story, the young man and Robbie walked to our school for English classes. They passed some parents who were playing with their small children, picking them up and laughing with them. The young man looked away suddenly and wiped a tear from his eye.

Robbie reflected on people from opposite sides of a conflict finding themselves together at Jubilee: "They knew that back in their own country they would have loved to have had the chance to kill each other, simply because they believed in what they were fighting for. But while they were here they got to see those people whom they had been against for so long in a different way. They sat in the same English classes with them, ate at table together when the whole community gathered, and worshiped together. Their consciences began to bother them about what they had done in their own country."

By the early 1980s, the U.S. government was shifting much of its attention in Central America to Nicaragua. For decades, the United States had supported the Somoza dynasty and its brutal National Guard. But in July 1979, the broadly supported Sandinista National Liberation Front dethroned the last ruling Somoza. Reversing a decades-long priority of catering to the appetites of a small elite, the Sandinistas launched a highly successful literacy campaign and dramatically improved health care and working conditions across Nicaragua.

In Washington, the triumph of the Sandinista revolution was viewed as a serious blow to U.S. dominance in Central America. When Ronald Reagan took over the presidency in January 1981, Jimmy Carter's human rights policies and diplomatic overtures toward the Sandinistas were quickly replaced with an unequivocal campaign against the Nicaraguan government.

U.S. money and equipment transformed the defeated National Guard troops, most of whom had fled to neighboring Honduras, into a serious fighting force. Using the same methods of terror they had employed under Somoza, these "counterrevolutionaries," or "Contras," began launching raids into Nicaragua, trying to reestablish a foothold on Nicaraguan soil.

One of their early targets was the town of Jalapa, located on the Honduran border. In February 1984, I stood on the seat beside the driver of a large truck as it bumped its way over a dirt road toward the tiny, isolated town. With the upper part of my body extended through an opening in the roof of the cab, I scanned the road ahead for signs of recent digging. The Contras had been planting land mines on this road. The driver was prepared to come to a screeching halt if I pounded on the roof.

I was a co-leader of a delegation sponsored by the Fellowship of Reconciliation, an international religious pacifist organization, and Witness for Peace, a nonviolent effort that maintained a U.S. presence in Nicaragua's war zones, offering protection and support to its vulnerable citizens.

We went to the very edge of Nicaragua and walked out to the center of a field between the Sandinista forces on one side and the Contra troops on the other. For half an hour we prayed under a banner that said, "Oramos por la Paz"—"We Pray for Peace." As we walked from the field back into the village of Teotecacente, a small woman approached us.

"I am Carmen Gutierrez," she said, "and I want to thank you for your prayers for peace. We need peace very much. Let me tell you what has happened to my family."

Six months earlier, Carmen and her children had been right where we were now standing when the Contras launched a mortar attack from across the field. The first mortar exploded at the edge of the yard, knocking them all to the ground. When they could, they plunged into the safety of a crude bomb shelter dug in the yard. But then Carmen realized that four-year-old Suyapa was missing.

Carmen looked out and saw that her daughter's body was all but decapitated by shrapnel. Weeping, she huddled with her other three children in the shelter for three grueling days while the attack continued and her daughter's little body lay on the ground above them. Carmen later planted a tiny plot of flowers on that spot.

That conversation with Carmen became one of the most important turning points in my life. I returned to Nicaragua again and again in the following years. Friendships I made there have lasted for decades.

A month after that first trip, I was back in Nicaragua looking for a site where we could establish the first Habitat for Humanity project in that country. Jimmy Carter was just about to begin his work with Habitat for Humanity, and he had a special interest in Nicaragua. He had asked that I come to his home to brief him as soon as I returned from this trip.

For the first project, we chose the poverty-stricken village of German Pomares in western Nicaragua. The existing houses were primitive thatched shelters in which animals ran in and out at will and people slept in homemade cots made of feedbags wrapped around poles, raised just high enough off the ground to discourage snakes from climbing into bed with them. I endured a sleepless night in one of these after a small pig and a goose got into an extraordinarily noisy fight directly under my cot.

Our old friends, Julie Knop and Jim and Sarah Hornsby, became the first Habitat leaders in Nicaragua. Thanks to them and to thousands of hardworking visitors and Nicaraguans, that little beginning led to more than 30,000 people living today in Habitat houses in Nicaragua. The German Pomares site received the first of many visits by Jimmy and Rosalynn Carter to Habitat projects outside the United States. Today a permanent branch office of the Carter Center operates in Nicaragua.

Early on the morning of October 20, 1986, I was at the Atlanta airport with several Habitat leaders, pastors, and reporters, ready to lead another delegation to Nicaragua. As our flight took off and Atlanta dropped away below us, an old truck was lumbering along a dirt road 1,500 miles to the south, headed for the small town of Jinotega in north-central Nicaragua.

Standing, seated on bags of grain on their way to market, and perched precariously on top of the truck's cab were fifty-one people. Among them was shy nineteen-year-old Carmen, who was on a joyful mission of preparation for her upcoming wedding. Her sister Cristina was there with her husband Amancio Sanchez, a thirty-year-old pastor who was heading to Jinotega to help plan a prayer vigil for peace. Several of their children were crowded into the truck as well, including seven-year-old Elda, a lively little girl with large brown eyes and a mischievous smile.

Just as the sun began to rise, the truck hit a land mine. The explosion blew a hole three feet deep into the road, hurling people and truck debris in all directions. Four of the passengers were killed instantly, and two more died on the way to the hospital. Forty-three others were seriously injured. Amancio lost his right leg in the explosion. Elda lay unconscious in a hospital for almost two weeks, one leg blown off at the knee and the other broken in eight places. Carmen lost both her legs. Her wedding never took place; her fiancé never came to see her again.

Their story was the major news story in Nicaragua while our delegation was there. That explosion would shape not only the rest of our stay but also much of Jubilee's work for years to come. My last night in Nicaragua on that fateful trip, I tossed restlessly. I got out of bed at about four o'clock in the morning and prayed in the darkness. During those moments, the Walk in Peace campaign was born—the first project of which was to bring the battered little Sanchez family to the United States to help them walk again. As it turned out, they became the first of thousands of Nicaraguans who have been helped through Walk in Peace.

On the way home, our group stopped at a heavily guarded compound in Tegucigalpa, Honduras, where I had arranged a meeting with Contra leaders at their headquarters. The place was eerily lit with floodlights and surrounded by concertina wire, and I remembered with irony that it was Halloween night back in the United States. This felt far scarier.

For two hours we met with the attorney general of the largest branch of the Contras, and Adela, the public relations officer. Chain-smoking and intense throughout our meeting, they did their best to convince us that the Contras were just and heroic. We confronted them with the many eyewitness accounts we had heard that indicated otherwise.

Adela, whose father had been a wealthy cotton grower and Somoza supporter, spoke nostalgically of her childhood and sadly of the scattering of her family after the triumph of the revolution. Before we left, I had a chance to speak with her privately outside her home. I told her that I thought she was wrong in her belief that the Nicaraguan people were waiting to welcome the Contras as their liberators. But then I stressed that I also felt the pain about her family she had described. I apologized for my country's part in their struggle.

Adela stood silently, staring intently at me, for several awkward moments. Then her eyes filled with tears, and she choked out, "Pray for me, and I will pray for you." She turned and rushed back into the house. I had not expected that my chief emotion of the evening would be pity for the "enemy," the very people who were causing such horrendous suffering just across the border.

Two weeks before, a teenage Nicaraguan soldier had shot down a U.S. C-123 cargo plane that was delivering arms and ammunition to the Contras. The only survivor, Eugene Hasenfus, parachuted into the arms of Nicaraguan troops. His trial began on November 15, the same day that I was back in Jinotega making arrangements to bring Carmen and the Sanchez family to the United States.

Hasenfus was sentenced in a Nicaraguan court to thirty years in prison, but that news was soon followed with the announcement that he would be set free. I heard this in a little plaza in the center of Jinotega, where I had sat down next to an older woman with a broad smile but few teeth. Her husband had been kidnapped by the Contras six months earlier, and she had feared that he was dead. But three weeks before our conversation, he had managed to escape and return to her. "Life was very hard while he was gone," she told me. "But now I thank God for his great mercy to my husband."

When I heard that the Sandinistas were releasing Eugene Hasenfus, I commented that that was likely to make a lot of Nicaraguans furious. "Oh, I think almost everyone will like it," the woman said. A man overhearing her nodded in agreement. I told them I didn't understand. With a look of patient amusement, the woman said, "Well, of course, it is almost Christmas, don't you see? It is a good time for him to be home with his family."

I had never heard such compassion for one's enemy expressed in such a matter-of-fact way. It was unthinkable to me that we in the United States would have done and felt the same if the roles had been reversed. News reports stated that Sandinista leaders had chosen to regard Hasenfus as a victim of U.S. policy rather than as a true enemy of the Nicaraguan people. But it was still startling to see Nicaraguan president Daniel Ortega shake his hand during the release ceremony.

With Jimmy Carter's help in acquiring their visas, Carmen and the Sanchez family arrived at the Atlanta airport on February 7, 1987. Staff at the Emory Center for Rehabilitative Medicine donated their skill and time, and friends of Jubilee paid for the family's prostheses. With the help of some members of Congress,

I organized a press conference in Washington to draw attention to the 2,000 amputees at the time who were, to a large extent, the victims of our government's Nicaragua policy. I announced the launching of the Walk in Peace campaign to help those on both sides of the conflict who needed artificial limbs. Most of these victims were villagers who had lost arms and legs to land mines or munitions manufactured and supplied by the United States.

At the press conference, Carmen sat in her wheelchair, an afghan hiding the pitiful remains of what had so recently been the strong legs of a beautiful young woman anticipating her wedding. Elda crawled into her mother's lap, the stump of her destroyed leg protruding from her skirt. With dignity and composure, Amancio stood before a phalanx of microphones and a wall of cameras and bright lights and related their tragic story.

He was risking his life to do so, knowing that the Contras could easily target him when he returned home. "Don, I am a dead man now," he told me soberly as soon as the room had cleared. Several of the reporters had been harsh and insistent with their questions, many filing reports that echoed the U.S. government's line implying that the Sandinistas had set the land mines and blamed the Contras.

A week later, the family was back at Jubilee, and Amancio and Elda were ready to be fitted for their prosthetic legs. Amancio said at breakfast that morning, "This will be one of the greatest days of my life—like the day I got married or the day I became a Christian. I will be able to walk again!" Carmen's turn came a few weeks later. The broad and beatific smiles on their faces as they took their first steps on their new legs were the most beautiful I imagine I'll ever see. Through the Walk in Peace program, over the years since that day we have helped to bring smiles to the faces of many other Nicaraguan amputees.

In November 1993, I returned to Nicaragua again. Though the Sandinistas had lost the national election in 1990 to Violeta

Chamorro, the U.S.-supported candidate, powerful members of the U.S. Congress continued to do all they could to strangle the Nicaraguan economy. The unemployment rate in Nicaragua was over 60 percent. The per capita income had fallen to the equivalent of less than one U.S. dollar per day. Masses of people crowded around our car at intersections, trying to sell pitiful little handfuls of chewing gum or trinkets, and boys clambered up on the hoods of cars to wash windshields, begging to be paid a coin or two.

The delegation members with me were struggling not to be overwhelmed by the apparent helplessness of it all. There was little enthusiasm when I announced that we would spend our last evening in one of Managua's poorest barrios, Batahola Norte. More than 10,000 people are crammed into houses jammed one against the other along its narrow dirt streets.

We entered a church, open on three sides and giving free passage to birds during services. Bright murals covered the other buildings in the church compound, and children were playing musical instruments: young girls producing a cacophony of squeaks on their plastic flutes, a boy so engrossed in his French horn that he didn't notice the group of foreign visitors, and two young musicians in a courtyard receiving lessons on cellos. Within minutes, our fatigue and discouragement lifted on this little island of beauty and hope in a sea of hardship. When the children sang for us, my eyes would not stay dry. I decided that people back home needed to hear this.

Months later, after lots of hard work and struggle on our part to obtain funding and visas, forty-one beaming young Nicaraguans arrived for a U.S. concert tour, with their leader, Fr. Angel Torrellas, repeating over and over, "A miracle! This is a miracle!" For eighteen days, they toured the eastern United States, giving twenty-eight concerts and receiving standing ovations at every stop for their folkloric dancing in colorful costumes and poignant singing. On the steps of the U.S. Capitol, just yards from the conference room where Amancio Sanchez had been grilled a few months earlier, they closed their concert with an act of gentle defiance. They sang a song of love for their country, "Nicaragua, Nicaraguita" ("Nicaragua, My Little Nicaragua").

In mid-May 1995, Amancio was again riding in the back of a truck on a rough mountain road in Nicaragua. Again preparations were being made for a wedding, this time for Amancio's oldest daughter, who was planning to marry the truck's young driver. The truck hit a large hole and skidded off the road. Amancio was thrown from the back and was crushed when the truck rolled over him. More than a thousand people gathered for this beloved pastor's funeral, carrying his body two miles to the cemetery in a massive procession.

Earlier that year I had learned that the Batahola Norte students were unable to attend college for lack of about $250 a year for tuition. We launched another fundraising campaign, enabling all twenty-seven of the high school graduates that year to go on for further education. Among the contributions were many from students in the U.S. who had met the young Nicaraguans on their concert tour. The students were generous when they realized that dozens of Nicaraguans could receive a college education for the equivalent of what just one student spends here. Thanks to the love of many of our friends, hundreds of young Nicaraguans have since been enabled to complete high school and college. Many of them are now providing leadership in programs that help their younger brothers and sisters.

Through the years, our connections with Nicaragua have continued to grow. We launched a major relief effort after hurricane Joan ravaged the country in 1988, and we sent Jubilee resident partners Sue and Blake Byler-Ortman and their family there for five months after hurricane Mitch wreaked its devastation a decade later. In the summer of 2005, our Jubilee teenagers made a trip that included a visit with Carmen and Elda. Elda had grown from a smiling child into a twenty-five-year-old teacher at a church-run school for children who cannot afford to attend public schools.

We have watched as more and more Central Americans, including now many Mexicans, have streamed into our country. According to our dear Nicaraguan friend Dr. Gustavo Parajón, "Our small farmers cannot compete with imports produced by huge agribusinesses elsewhere. With an unemployment rate of sixty percent, our people stand in line outside sweatshops to compete for jobs that pay them only a few cents per hour as they manufacture goods to be sold in the United States." He stated his belief that the twenty-first century really began when the Soviet Union collapsed and we in United States were able to turn our full attention to economic domination of the rest of the world.

Over the years, we at Jubilee have been involved in many other peace and justice efforts. We helped coordinate a national protest against shipments of hundreds of nuclear weapons on the "White Train," involving several midnight chases of trains through the southern United States. We've vigiled at the gates of the School of the Americas at Fort Benning, Georgia, now called the Western Hemisphere Institute for Security Cooperation, demanding its closure because of its history of training Latin American military officers in tactics of torture and repression. We've refused to pay the portion of our personal income taxes used for war, pitting us in a battle with the IRS and sending a few of us to jail. We've made countless visits to prisoners on death row and publicly protested capital punishment. We sent several delegations to renovate houses in southern Mississippi in the wake of hurricane Katrina, and have confronted the racism of the Ku Klux Klan locally.

But the flow of refugees through Jubilee Partners has always been the lifeblood of our community. Through the years, as thousands of people from dozens of countries have lived among us, we have been consistently awed by their resilience of spirit and humbled by their gratitude and love. We are reminded every day that Jesus began his life as a refugee—that his birth so threatened King Herod that it led to the mass slaughter of innocent children and his family's flight to Egypt. We have seen Jesus come among us again and again in many guises.

One of the best parts of our work is watching people from diverse cultural backgrounds become good friends. Just as violence of one group against another requires first that people distance themselves from one another, so peacemaking involves overcoming distances—learning to talk with one another, share food, play and laugh together. We have watched many people, including ourselves, move beyond the harmful rhetoric based on fear, racism, and greed that is so common in our country.

The poignancy of the connections between us was brought home when Joe Mulligan was executed by the state of Georgia. He was from a large African American family, and his minister refused to bury him because of his crime. We agreed to lay him to rest in our simple Jubilee cemetery.

Joe's family came dressed in their finest. The awkwardness was written on their faces as they arrived, no doubt wondering what kind of strange place they had come to in order to bury their loved one. But we all started down the road together, carrying Joe's body. From time to time, someone would tap another person on the shoulder and say, "Let me take the load now." We became a community united in dignity and sorrow.

The Central Americans who were with us then joined the solemn procession. We hadn't told them much about the circumstances of Joe's death. But one commented, "The power that killed this man made us flee our homes. The power that killed this man killed our relatives, too." Joe's family nodded their heads, saying, "Yes."

The Central Americans insisted on helping us dig the grave. Most of them had not been able to do that for their own loved ones. The ground at Jubilee is rocky, and digging a grave requires arduous labor with a pickax. The Central Americans gave it their full effort, sending sparks flying off the rocks we were trying to break. "This is for my mother," one would say in Spanish. "This is for my brother." They named a litany of people who had died or been executed in El Salvador, one name for each swing of the ax. They knew what it meant to be executed by the state.

Over and over again we have been moved by the witnesses to reconciliation and compassion for enemies who come among us. Mana, a Muslim woman of Albanian descent, had been a nurse in Sarajevo for thirteen years. She found it impossible to leave her patients. With great anguish, she sent her five-year-old son, Admir, to safety with her brother in neighboring Croatia. Little Admir cried as his mother put him on the train. "Mama, sit here. Look, there is a place for you. Come with us!" he pleaded, tears spilling out of his eyes. As the train pulled away, Mana also wept, knowing she might never see her son again.

For months Mana walked the two-and-a-half miles from her home to the hospital every day, crossing a market that was the site of a massacre and dodging the bullets of snipers. "They would shoot at anything that moved—soldiers, civilians, animals, anything," she said. The hospital was an oasis of good will in a desert of ethnic warfare. "We took care of everyone," Mana explained, "Muslims, Serbs, and Croats, even some of the Serb soldiers taken by our men. No one could touch them when they were in our care."

Sometimes her patients would receive packages of food from their relatives in Serbia and share them with the hospital staff. "The soldiers were shooting at us, and their mothers were sharing their food with us," she said. "These people were victims, too, and suffering with us.

"If a person is sick, if she can't walk, I don't have the heart to say, 'See what your people are doing?' How can I do that? I must help her," Mana said. Of her loss of home and possessions, Mana reflected, "I lost all those things in five seconds. Love is permanent. Things are nothing."

Finally, after three years, Mana could not stay apart from her son anymore, and she went to him. Admir did not recognize her, insisting that his mother was much younger and more beautiful. "I was also surprised," she admitted. "I was expecting a small boy. He had grown so tall." They had a happy ending and a deepened connection as mother and son at Jubilee.

In recent years we have welcomed many refugees from the war-torn and famine-ridden areas of Africa. Mabel Johnson fled from Liberia with her children in 1992, when her youngest son, Diamond, "was only bones," she said. In Nigeria, Mabel was followed and beaten by Liberian rebel forces, who threatened to kill her. She decided to undertake a forty-day fast. In a dream, she was told to compose a letter pleading for asylum, which she later wrote and delivered to the U.S. embassy.

"The Lord took me from the trash and put me on a silver platter!" she exclaimed at Jubilee. "It was nothing but a miracle." While she was sharing her story with us, the people of Ebenezer Baptist Church in Atlanta, where Dr. Martin Luther King had served, were making the decision to sponsor Mabel and her family. When she got the news the next morning, she thanked God for yet another miracle: "I know only the power of the Holy Spirit saved our lives."

In 1999 the Thomas family—Olayinka, Philip, and their five children—escaped from Sierra Leone, which had been shattered by a military coup, an insurgency of guerilla fighters, and international greed focused on its diamond mines. The country had collapsed into a general state of brutality in which thousands of people—even tiny babies—had been maimed or killed. Olayinka both criticized the government and appealed to the guerillas via television to "leave the children out of it." As a result, she received death threats from both sides.

At Jubilee, we asked her children what would make the world a better place. "Stop war," said Ishma, 16. His sister Lango, 14, added, "War destroys the lifetime of children. It takes away our future." Olayinka said of her children, "I don't want them to be hard as the world is hard."

The Bantus of Somalia are subsistence farmers who have been treated as virtual slaves for many generations. They too have been targeted by all sides in the chaotic fighting in their country, and they received brutal treatment from marauding bandits who followed them to U.N. refugee camps in Kenya. The first question of many when they arrived at Jubilee was, "Are there lions in the woods?" We assured them that there were no lions and no civil war around us.

"This country is very peaceful and very... decorated!" exclaimed Maalin, groping for a word to express the contrast between the barren desert from which he had just come and this land covered with so many trees, buildings, cars, and signs. More than any other group, the Somali Bantus were overwhelmed by the challenges of clocks and calendars, phones and money—and the miracle of a gas range with instant fire. But one man could recite his paternal lineage for twenty-four generations back, and we learned to appreciate the gifts of an oral, communal culture.

We got used to seeing women and girls strolling around our Welcome Center in bright African dresses of dazzling colors like butterflies, and to hearing the laughter of children riding their new bikes and playing together. At one point we had parents from Eritrea and Ethiopia walking and talking together, smiling. It didn't matter that their two nations were deadlocked in a bitter war. They were trying out their new language with one another, Africans proudly speaking English with a Georgia accent. One Ethiopian declared, "We are all one here."

We are pleased at Jubilee to have a soccer field with enough international competition to rival the Olympics. Every Thanksgiving brings a celebration with people from all over the world, a return of Jubilee "alumni" who show up in the garb of their native lands, bearing gifts of food for a sumptuous international feast. How privileged we are at Jubilee to be called to this ministry of hope and compassion! Whenever we're tempted to give in to weariness or frustration, we remember that our lives are so...decorated!

In 1999 we had among us Muslims fleeing the repressive Islamic fundamentalism of the Taliban in Afghanistan, other Muslims driven out by Christians in Bosnia, Iraqi Kurds fleeing persecution, and Christians who had survived the mass slaughter being carried out by Islamic leaders in Sudan. We asked two Muslim teenage brothers from Sudan what is most important in the world. Mohamed, 18, said, "Whatever difficulties we face, we must learn to understand each other and to live in peace." His seventeen-year-old brother, Walid, speaking softly and with deep feeling, said, "We just want people to love us."

As the twenty-first century has dawned, we have witnessed a growing gulf between Muslims and the West, fanned into flames by sensationalist media, the U.S. attacks on Iraq and Afghanistan, the retaliation of suicide bombers and many other deadly new techniques of surprise attack, and provocative practices such as the tortures at Abu Ghraib and Guantánamo. All the while the stakes are constantly being raised by the relentless proliferation of nuclear weapons and technology. In a time such as this, I am especially grateful for our calling. We discover over and over again how much all of us human beings share in common—needing love, wanting peace, and holding onto precious dreams.

Thirty years of working with refugees from all over the world has taught us that cultural barriers fall away quickly when we meet people face-to-face and learn to know them as human beings fundamentally like ourselves, as brothers and sisters all created by God. Our friend Jimmy Carter said it eloquently when he received the Nobel Peace Prize in 2002: "The bond of our common humanity is stronger than the divisiveness of our fears and prejudices. God gives us the capacity for choice. We can choose to alleviate suffering. We can choose to work together for peace. We can make these changes—and we must."

Ah, but it is one thing to be convinced that we should work for peace—and altogether another thing to know *how*. We became more and more determined to find answers to that question.

CHAPTER THREE

No Time to Waste

T all and gracious in manner, Sougui Adji reflected his aristocratic background. His grandfather had been the chief of the Teda people, almost a million of whom live in Chad, Niger, and Libya. His uncle had served as president of Chad from 1979 to 1982. Sougui and his wife, Ache, came to Jubilee in 2007, already speaking fluent English and always happy to stop whatever he was doing to engage in conversation.

Sougui proved to be a treasure trove of information about northern Africa. A Muslim who had experienced long years of friendship with Christians in Africa, he was able to bridge many cultures with ease. Consequently, he had served as advisor and guide to National Geographic Society projects and to other groups that came to make documentary films or do research for books about the region.

Chad lies in the center of one of the world's most dramatic examples of climate change in recent years. The northern part of the country is classic Saharan desert: vast stretches of sand and rock, broken at rare intervals by oases with their precious water supply. The capital city, N'Djamena, lies at the southern end of what used to be Lake Chad. In the early 1960s, the lake covered 10,000 square miles—the ultimate oasis in the middle of the world's largest desert.

If you have a computer with Google Earth, I urge you to zoom in on Lake Chad and take a look at it now. Few sights anywhere on earth illustrate the effects of climate change more dramatically. After forty years of diminished rainfall throughout the region and ever-greater concentrations of nomadic people depending on it for their water needs, the lake has shrunk to barely one-twentieth its former size. In a short time, barring a miraculous reversal of climate trends, it will be totally dry.

Sougui has watched this change happen during his lifetime. He remembers as a small boy seeing the northern edge of Africa's equatorial jungle extending all the way up to N'Djamena. Thirty years later, he drove all day across that same region south of the city—across the almost bare sands of the expanding desert. He told me of similar situations all over Chad; many oases in the north have dried up and disappeared.

"So, of course the people are competing with each other for water now," Sougui said sadly. "Their crops will not grow. Their animals have no grass. There is no fuel with which to cook their food. What can they do? They migrate—and they end up fighting with other people who need the same water. It is a very big problem."

Many of those displaced farmers and other migrants are from just across the border in Sudan. A family of refugees from Darfur in western Sudan came through Jubilee recently. The mother looked around at our green meadows and forest and sighed, "Jubilee is so beautiful. It reminds me of Darfur was when I was a girl."

Now Darfur has become a parched wasteland of warring ethnic groups. Even the thousands of U.N. soldiers and police deployed there are unable to give adequate protection to the millions of suffering people caught up in its horror. Their historic differences of religion, race, and politics have been pushed to the point of bloody conflict by their shared struggle for food and water.

In the southeastern United States, we have also suffered a

shortage of rainfall in the past few years. The greater Atlanta area, already more than 5 million in population and one of the fastest-growing urban areas in the country, has serious water problems these days. I've stopped counting the number of front-page articles in the *Atlanta Journal-Constitution* about our state legislature's embarrassing proposals to address the problem by trying to force Tennessee to supply water for Georgia residents. Or about the "water wars" between Georgia, Alabama, and Florida over how to share the dwindling Chattahoochee River. The drought became so severe in November 2007 that Georgia's governor, Sonny Perdue, led a prayer service for rain on the steps of the Capitol Building—on a rare cloudy day.

All the while, the residents of Atlanta and of the nation as a whole have continued to consume an average of about 100 gallons of water per capita every day through our public water systems. This is in addition to nearly 500 gallons per capita each day used for irrigation in this country—most of it going to grow feed for the production of beef, pork, and poultry. No politician wants to challenge seriously the notion that we can continue to use such huge amounts of the shrinking supply of fresh water.

"How does that compare with water usage by the people of Chad?" I asked Sougui.

"Many of our people live on as little as five liters a day," he answered, "for drinking, cooking, bathing, everything." That equals 1.3 gallons. That means that, on average, each person in this country personally uses as much water as a whole village in Chad!

More important—and more directly relevant to the changing climate—is the fact that we in the United States have become energy gluttons. We use more energy per person, on average, than just about any other nation on earth—much more in total consumption than any other with a population close to the size of ours. (The Canadians are close, but they can at least argue that more energy is necessary to heat their homes during their colder winters.) We make up only 4.5 percent of the world's population, but we consume close to one-quarter of all the energy being produced on this planet.

If most or all of that energy came from "green" sources, such as solar power, wind, or geothermal energy, this would not be such a problem. But the fact is that about 86 percent of the energy used in the United States comes from oil, coal, and natural gas— all fossil fuels that produce "greenhouse gases" and contribute to global warming. A few years ago, there may have been room for debate about whether we and the other big energy consumers are endangering life on Earth. That debate has all but ended now, except among a few die-hard skeptics or people who are so committed to short-term convenience or profit that they are willing to sacrifice future generations.

Late in 2007, the American Geophysical Union—the world's largest professional society of earth and space scientists— adopted a strong statement on "Human Impacts on Climate." It begins,

> The Earth's climate is now clearly out of balance and is warming. Many components of the climate system—including the temperatures of the atmosphere, land and ocean, the extent of sea ice and mountain glaciers, the sea level, the distribution of precipitation, and the length of seasons—are now changing at rates and in patterns that are not natural and are best explained by the increased atmospheric abundances of greenhouse gases and aerosols generated by human activity.

Just prior to that, in an article published in *The Washington Post* titled "Starving the People to Feed the Cars," Earth Policy Institute president Lester Brown gave special attention to the way our insatiable thirst for oil in the United States is a major factor in the emerging hunger crisis. With oil reserves shrinking rapidly and the price of petroleum climbing, an ever-larger portion of agricultural products is being converted to ethanol to supplement the oil supply. "The grain required to fill a 25-gallon SUV gas tank with ethanol would feed one person for a full year," wrote Brown. "If the United States converted its entire grain harvest into ethanol, it would satisfy less than 16 percent of its automotive fuel needs."[1]

In his excellent book *Plan B 3.0: Mobilizing to Save Civilization,* Brown describes the global food and energy relationship in detail. He explains that in six of the past seven years, world grain consumption has exceeded production. As a result, the world's grain reserves are disappearing, prices are rising steeply, and millions of the world's poorest people are facing the prospect of mass starvation if something does not change very soon.[2]

Gwynne Dyer takes these themes a step further in his newest book, *Climate Wars.* Presenting one frightening scenario after another as he explores the way climate interacts with economics, politics, food supply, violence born of desperation, and other factors, Dyer argues that "for every degree the average global temperature rises, so do the mass movements of population, the number of failed and failing states, and very probably the incidence of internal and international wars. Which, if they become big and frequent enough, will sabotage the global cooperation that is the only way to stop the temperature from continuing to climb."[3]

Sougui's firsthand report from the Sahara Desert reflects what is starting to happen around the world. The United Nations has reported that, as of about 2003, the number of "environmental refugees" has surpassed even the growing number of political and war-related refugees in the world. Huge numbers of people are being displaced either by too little water in some places (diminishing supplies) or too much water in others (rising sea levels and storm surges).

Some experts say that such factors already drive up to 10 million people from their homes each year. Predictably, the response by many skeptics to such warnings has been to dismiss the displaced people as (merely) "economic refugees" looking for a better life—especially those who happen to be coming into the United States.

Indeed, this is a complex matter. How does one sort out the exact relationship of environmental degradation, economic collapse, hunger, and political breakdown? Certainly the majority of the thousands of refugees who have come through Jubilee have suffered from most, if not all, of these catastrophes. They can usually point to particular calamities that made their situations worse, but even they cannot grasp all the complex factors that led to their suffering and drove them from the homes and families they love.

Early in 2007, I had the privilege of going through three days of intensive training in one of former Vice President Al Gore's special workshops on climate change. We participants received a wealth of background information to help us spread the word that the problem of global warming is profoundly important—and that it is indeed still possible to avoid global catastrophe.

The equivalent of a good college science course was packed into those three days. For me the highlight was one simple point that Gore made during the second day: "Most people in your audiences will probably be in denial about this stuff. If you come along and simply drive them out of denial and into despair, you will have just made the situation worse. Neither condition leads to meaningful action. You must help them to understand why there is hope—*but only if we go out and do something about it!*"

Denial about the state of the world becomes impossible when the survivors of war and famine and environmental ruin show up on the doorstep. The refugees who come through Jubilee Partners are an inspiring reminder to us that hope can be found in even the most catastrophic and overwhelming situations. Over the years they have arrived straight from epic struggles for survival that rival the drama in blockbuster movies. Against the greatest odds, they have lived through some of the world's worst tragedies. We have found their faith and their commitment to helping one another along the way deeply humbling.

One inspiring example among many is Paula Balegamire, one of the most courageous women I have ever met. She is from the city of Bukavu in the eastern part of the Democratic Republic of the Congo (DRC). The Second Congo War, also known as the Great War of Africa, lasted from 1998 to 2003 and directly involved eight African nations that are increasingly competing for resources. It was the deadliest conflict since World War II, claiming the lives of 5.4 million people in the fighting and the disease and starvation that were rampant in its aftermath.

During the war, when a conflict between ethnic groups broke out, Paula's husband, Joseph, was across the country in the capital city of Kinshasa. Hostile armies and a thousand miles of jungle separated him from Paula and their five small children. Surrounded by danger, Paula managed to escape and take the children through Tanzania, Rwanda, Burundi, and Zambia. After an arduous and extremely perilous journey, she and Joseph were reunited in Kinshasa.

Not long afterward, however, the DRC's President Kabila began to round up men from the eastern part of the country, suspecting anyone from there of being a threat to him and his government. Paula, Joseph, and the children escaped across the Congo River into Brazzaville. But then Joseph was caught and imprisoned, along with about sixty other men from his region. Over the next few months, half of them were executed.

Paula, by that time pregnant with their sixth child and again hemmed in by danger, was determined to save her children. She gave birth to Gloria in 2001. She managed somehow to keep the children together and alive for the next three years, until finally the family was granted refugee status and flown to the United States.

Paula and her six children arrived at Jubilee Partners in November 2004. At that time, a thousand people a day were dying of malnutrition and disease in the DRC. Watching the children enjoy the first welcome they had ever received in a safe place was a special thrill for us.

Paula and her children became a beautiful part of our life. The older boys especially loved soccer, and all the kids rode bicycles up and down the Jubilee road, celebrating their new freedom of movement and safety. Paula's face glowed as she sang in our worship services. At one point, she danced into our school building with joy after seeing Gloria smile for the first time in her stressful little life. "Gloria smiled! Gloria smiled!" she repeated over and over.

Meanwhile, Joseph continued to be in grave danger in the prison in Africa. But at long last the wonderful news came that he was out of jail and back in Brazzaville. He found a cell phone and contacted Paula. He was free for the moment, but he had very little money. His danger was by no means over, and he had to find some way to escape from the crosscurrents of fighting groups.

Bill and Sabra Reichardt, good friends of Jubilee, agreed to give $1,000 to help Joseph survive and seek political asylum. The challenge was getting it to him. But Paula was determined, and by then she was an expert at such things. One night she even managed to set up a call between Joseph—speaking from his hiding place on his precious cell phone—and me. Since most of the conversation was in French and mine is extremely poor, their oldest son was on the line with us as interpreter.

We got the money to Joseph, who used it to survive while the United Nations High Commissioner for Refugees (UNHCR) considered his appeal. In January 2008, the joyful news arrived that he had finally been flown to safety in Europe. Paula, the epitome of faith and courage in action, was absolutely ecstatic! Her prayers had been answered. She flew to Europe for the joyful reunion, taking seven-year-old Gloria with her to meet her father for the very first time!

How could we live daily in a stream of such heroic survivors and not be inspired? They have been our rescuers from denial, constantly reminding us of the suffering of people around the world, stirring us to hope, and moving us to take action to end violence, economic exploitation, and the ravages of climate change. Over and over, we have been strengthened by the example of their faith and their courage—qualities needed now more than ever, as the plight of refugees around the world continues to grow worse.

The number of officially recognized refugees continues to escalate, outrunning all the efforts of the UNHCR and international refugee support groups to resettle them. Most of these organizations focus their efforts on "political refugees." These are, by definition, the people who have been forced by a "well-founded fear of persecution" to leave their own countries in order to find safety. According to the United States Committee on Refugees (USCR), more than 14 million people are now in this category.

That is a tragedy on a grand scale in itself, but another trend makes it still worse: the "warehousing" of refugees. This is the term used for the increasingly common situation in which displaced people are left in camps for many years rather than being resettled in other countries. When we started our work at Jubilee Partners in 1979, Palestinians made up the great majority of refugees who seemed to be trapped in no-exit situations that generated enormous amounts of anger and frustration. Many had already been waiting as many as thirty years in countries such as Lebanon, Jordan, and Egypt for some resolution of their status. Now they have been there twice as long.

The next large population to be "warehoused" in this way was the Afghans. In the early 1980s, they were trapped mostly in squalid border settlements in Pakistan and Iran. Since then, people from many countries have met a similar fate. Often they are barely surviving under terrible conditions. Almost always they are prohibited from seeking employment. Year after year their number grows.

Today, more than 8.5 million refugees have been trapped in such camps and "temporary" settlements for ten years or more. Many people have come to us from Africa after waiting well over a decade in very restrictive camps in Kenya or Tanzania. Some of the refugees who have come through Jubilee most recently—driven out of the battered little country known as both Myanmar and Burma—have languished in camps for up to twenty years.

To state the obvious, this spreading practice of neglecting millions of refugees causes great frustration among them and creates perfect incubators for violent extremists. How could it not do so? Imagine if all the citizens of, say, Georgia or New Jersey (which have populations about equal to the number of people who have now been "warehoused" for ten years or more) were penned up in squalid camps crowded with makeshift huts, cut off from travel and work, given just enough food for day-to-day survival, and provided with little or no medical or educational support. How long could we expect that situation to last without a violent response of some kind? After ten or fifteen years of such hopeless living, how would our young people be likely to respond if recruiters from some violent militia group or terrorist organization offered them an alternative?

I long for the day when every church congregation in the United States that claims to follow Jesus clamors to have the privilege of sponsoring at least one of these refugee families! The churches themselves would be tremendously blessed, and the suffering in those "warehouse" camps would be drastically reduced. What if...?

Recorded in the twenty-fifth chapter of the Gospel of Matthew is this command from Jesus to his followers: "Give food to the hungry and water to the thirsty, take the stranger into your home, clothe the naked, go to the aid of the sick and those in prison." Jesus made clear that serving those in such need was the same as caring for Jesus himself: "Just as you did it to one of the least of these who are members of my family, you did it to me" (Matthew

25:40, NRSV). I think we can safely guess that today he would add a clear word concerning our consumptive—and increasingly destructive—relationship toward everything around us in this beautiful creation we were given.

To turn our faces from refugees and dismiss them all as economic opportunists is not only to display a cold indifference toward our struggling brothers and sisters, it is also to practice an almost pathological level of denial of the global trends that threaten all of us. The peril of environmental collapse is hurtling down the road toward even those who, for the moment, may have a greater problem with being overweight than with facing starvation.

We are not only among those most responsible for this crisis, we are the ones still most able to take effective action. We can cut our waste dramatically, break our addiction to oil and coal, turn to the green technologies that are already fully available, change our eating habits—and open our hearts to the people struggling now to survive on this little planet, as well as to our own children and future generations. Or we can continue as in the past. And, perhaps within another decade or two, according to many experts, we will discover that we have crossed the threshold into irreversible global catastrophe. There is, quite literally, no time left to waste!

CHAPTER FOUR

Aid and Comfort

It was March 1991, and I was standing in the burnt and twisted remains of a building in the Ameriya district of Baghdad. The room was eerily lit by the sun's rays, filtering down from a hole blasted through six feet of reinforced concrete. Hundreds of civilians had been killed here—mostly women and children, and a few elderly men—when two U.S. "smart bombs" struck the roof a few weeks before. The tragedy had happened on February 13, Ash Wednesday.

Fifty-three charred bodies were removed the first day, more than ninety the second, then a ghastly stream of others for many days thereafter. I was painfully conscious as I examined this dreadful place that I was standing in the ashes of hundreds of innocent people, on a street that some survivors had renamed "Street Without Women." I will never forget the anguish of one of the men we met, who in his torment shouted over and over at us, "My wife and children were destroyed by your great weapons. Why? What did they ever do to you?" Next to him, an old man stood silently, tears running down and dripping from his chin.

I was there a week after the U.S. bombing raids of the first Gulf War had ended, leading a delegation of reporters to try to find out the impact of the raids on the civilian population of Iraq. This part of the news had been deliberately and conspicuously kept from the American public by our leaders. When we got to Iraq, our hearts were broken by the widespread suffering, especially among the children. At the same time, we were utterly astonished by the spirit of most of the people we met who, despite their agony as a result of the attack by our country's forces, treated us warmly and hospitably.

While we were there, we visited several children's hospitals. The memory of some of those injured children, many of them screaming in pain, will be etched in my mind for the rest of my life. I returned from that trip resolved to find some way to help them.

In the years that followed, I spoke about what I had witnessed to hundreds of audiences in churches and universities all over the U.S. Mostly, but not always, I found people here eager to blame all the suffering on Saddam Hussein. Meanwhile, of course, he was blaming it all on our country's sanctions against Iraq. The truth, I believe, is that both sides were responsible. I was beginning to understand that we were partners with Saddam in this terrible punishment of millions of innocent Iraqi people.

For that 1991 trip, our delegation had tried unsuccessfully to take medicine to Iraq's children. We had collected thousands of dollars' worth of antibiotics, pain medication, and vaccines and hauled them to New York's JFK airport. There the U.S. authorities refused us permission to take them any farther. The medicine spoiled in a warehouse at the airport, while we visited Iraqi hospitals and stood empty-handed, watching children struggle to live. We were helpless as they looked at us with their dark eyes, large and full of pain, dying right in front of us for lack of simple medical supplies.

About the same time that we were in Iraq, a United Nations delegation was sent by the Secretary General to assess the situation there. Its members reported back that the war had "wrought near-apocalyptic results." They warned especially that the targeting of Baghdad's non-military structures, such as power plants, water treatment facilities, food processing plants, and sewage treatment facilities, would lead to "imminent catastrophe" for the civilian population, unless emergency measures were undertaken at once.

The sanctions had been put into place before the war by the United States to force Saddam Hussein to withdraw from Kuwait. After that objective had been achieved, however, they were continued (and even expanded in scope), with the new goal of forcing Saddam out of power altogether. I was in favor of genuine military sanctions against Saddam Hussein, carefully designed and administered. But the cruel and clumsy way we went about this for more than a decade caused a horrible amount of pain and death for the most vulnerable of Iraq's people. In the process, we made it easy for the dictator to use this as propaganda to embitter his people against the West and to strengthen his own grip on power.

Where could we ever find a better demonstration of the futility of using cruel, violent means to overcome evil? The more I learned about this whole terrible episode, the more convinced I became of that central teaching of Jesus that we must always seek ways to overcome evil with good (Matthew 5:43-48; compare Romans 12:21). But how do we do that? What could we do?

I was torn by these questions as the reports continued to come out of Iraq. The first Bush administration was followed by eight years of President Bill Clinton's leadership, then by President George W. Bush. The brutality of the sanctions continued to take their awful toll, whether Democrats or Republicans were in the White House. The problem was not just one of partisan politics. It was far more profound than that. It was rooted in our national faith in violence, our belief that we could solve problems by inflicting suffering on our enemies.

By 1996 an intense debate was under way about how many Iraqi civilians had died as a result of the economic sanctions, with some reports estimating that more than one million Iraqis had died as a direct consequence of this policy. There was constant, intense debate among the members of the U.N. Security Council about these matters, but the other nations' protests were trumped by the greater power of the United States. The sanctions remained in place—broad, cruel, and devastating, especially to the most helpless people of Iraq, the elderly and the very young.

In March 1996, the World Health Organization (WHO) reported that since the onset of sanctions, there had been a six-fold increase in the mortality rate for children under five and the majority of Iraq's population had been on a semi-starvation diet for years. The report concluded: "The psychological trauma of the six-week 1991 war and the terrible hardships enduring with the sanctions since then, can be expected to leave indelible marks on the mental health and behavioural patterns of [Iraq's] children when they grow to adulthood."[1]

Other reports from international health experts began to be published, describing epidemics of cholera, typhoid fever, and gastroenteritis in Iraq, especially among the children. The director of UNICEF stated that the collapse of the health system and the effects of the sanctions had contributed to the deaths of half a million children under the age of five since 1991, the time of my first visit to those broken pediatric hospitals in Baghdad.

At Jubilee we were deeply disturbed by these reports. Undoubtedly, our reaction to them was stronger than that of most people because of our daily work with beautiful refugee kids who had also suffered so much. We prayed and talked about the matter day after day. We all knew that peacemaking was at the heart of what Jesus had called his followers to do. If we were to love even our enemies, what possible justification could there be for causing the deaths of so many children? We had no illusions that we had all the answers or that whatever we might do would make any great difference in the overall course of events. But we knew we had to do something.

The thought kept running through my mind, "We act our way

into new ways of thinking more often than we think our way into new ways of acting." Surely, if we took at least some small steps to help relieve this suffering of the innocents, God would show us what to do next. If we acted on our desire to be faithful to Jesus' own example and put our compassion into practice, maybe we would gain new insights about the next steps. In any event, we decided we would rather risk failure while trying to be faithful to God than risk failure by our silent assent to this cruel policy being enforced primarily by our own government.

In February 1998, we took action. We sent out a newsletter with a call for our friends to help us save as many of those children as we could. With or without official permission from our government, we were going to buy as much medicine as possible and try to deliver it personally to the children's hospitals in Iraq.

We ended the newsletter with a "Prayer for Peace," in which we prayed for the leaders of both the United States and Iraq—as well as for Richard Butler, the man with perhaps the most delicate and difficult job in the world at that time. Butler was an Australian diplomat and head of the United Nations Special Commission on Iraq (UNSCOM). He and his team constantly raced around Iraq, searching for solid evidence of the "weapons of mass destruction" that Saddam was suspected of having produced and hidden somewhere. These weapons, if they existed, were the most frequent justification for the preparations by the United States for a second Gulf War.

Month after month passed, and—despite hundreds of surprise inspections by UNSCOM teams to sites all over Iraq—no "WMDs" were found. Meanwhile, Richard Butler walked an incredibly dangerous tightrope between Baghdad and Washington, in full view of the world's media day after day. The slightest mistake, tipping toward either side, could lead to disaster. We could think of no leader anywhere who needed our prayers more than he did.

I wish I could claim that we had no uncertainty about what we were doing. But we were painfully aware that many sincere people—even among those who usually applauded our work at Jubilee—would be offended by our actions. "After all," argued one man, "aren't you giving 'aid and comfort to the enemy' by such actions? That is a very serious step to take!"

"Of course it is," I responded. "But isn't that exactly what Jesus had in mind when he said that we should love our enemies instead of hating them? And what about Romans 12, where Paul says that we should give food to hungry enemies and water if they are thirsty? If that isn't 'aid and comfort,' what is? When Paul went on to say that we should 'overcome evil with good,' was he just being naïve? We think we can do more to make peace this way than through more and more violence."

To our relief and amazement, we found that the vast majority of people on our Jubilee mailing list felt the same way we did. The response to our newsletter was absolutely thrilling! Hundreds of letters poured into our office, almost all of them containing contributions to help us buy medicine. Along with thousands of dollars came many eloquent letters from people thanking us for giving them a tangible way to take action. We had touched a responsive chord among a lot of our fellow Christians.

We were further encouraged when many of our Muslim friends responded, some sending notes of encouragement as well as generous donations. These were refugees from Bosnia and Africa who had come through Jubilee after suffering in ways that helped them identify with the Iraqi children.

On March 20, 1998, Will Winterfeld and I set out from Jubilee to take the medicine into Iraq. Dr. Larry Willms, a Canadian physician who had served earlier as a volunteer at Jubilee, joined us on the way to Amman, Jordan. Friends there from the Mennonite Central Committee (MCC) had been busily collecting the medicine and preparing it for transport by truck into Iraq.

We had sent about $50,000 to them ahead of time. Buying from Turkish, Jordanian, and Egyptian pharmaceutical companies, our

Mennonite friends had managed to get several times more medicine and supplies than we would have been able to purchase with the same money in the United States. When we arrived in Amman, we were thrilled to find that they had filled five large trucks, each of them piled high with precious crates of lifesaving supplies. The Red Crescent (the Muslim equivalent of the Red Cross in Christian countries) supplied the drivers for the trucks.

We left Amman at four o'clock in the afternoon with a Palestinian driver named Samir. The highway to Baghdad was excellent most of the way, especially once we crossed into Iraq. There was no speed limit, so Samir drove his new Chevy Suburban at speeds of more than 100 miles per hour all the way. He explained that to drive at slower speeds was to invite trouble from bandits along the highway.

As we sped through the night, I could see that Samir was getting dangerously sleepy. With my own internal clock still half a dozen time zones back to the west, I was wide awake, to say the least—especially when once or twice I saw Samir's head nod and the car swerve. Samir quickly accepted my offer to take over the wheel, and minutes later he was asleep as I drove along the ancient caravan route. We crossed the Fertile Crescent at speeds at least thirty to forty times that of Abraham and Sarah and countless others who had followed this same route through the millennia. Eighteen hours after leaving Amman, we checked into the Al Rasheed Hotel in downtown Baghdad, totally exhausted.

After a good night of sleep, we set out for a series of diplomatic meetings with Iraqi health officials. Then we began delivering the medicine to the five pediatric hospitals on our list. In addition to the Red Crescent drivers, a representative from the Middle East Council of Churches went with us as guide and interpreter.

At every hospital, I was deeply impressed by the Iraqi doctors. They each deserved a Nobel Peace Prize, in my humble opinion. Most of them had been trained in the United States or the United Kingdom. Almost all of them spoke fluent English. They were intelligent and sophisticated. More important than that, they were obviously full of compassion for their little patients.

But they were also terribly frustrated. Working in facilities that were often dark (not enough light bulbs) and unsanitary (very little disinfectant), they improvised constantly (few functioning centrifuges, incubators, or other pieces of equipment). They kept records by hand (almost no working photocopy machines, computers, or even typewriters), often on the backs of pages from old medical files of patients they had already lost (very little new paper). They worked constantly with children struggling to breathe (no oxygen supplies) and moaning with pain (little or no anesthesia or even the most basic pain relievers). They had almost no nurses to help them (no money with which to pay them). With the collapsed economy of Iraq, the doctors themselves made so little money in the hospitals that they each had to work long hours at night in private practice to survive.

Dr. Selma Haddad was head of the cancer ward in one of the largest children's hospitals. She told me that the worst part of her work was that almost all her little patients die—for lack of medicine that would ordinarily cure at least 80 percent of them. I asked her how she kept from giving up.

"I have to keep on," Dr. Haddad answered with a sad smile. "There is no other alternative. I feel all these patients are my children. I'm feeling really sad for them. Their suffering is beyond description."

For this grim work, Dr. Haddad's salary was the equivalent of about eight dollars a month. By comparison, the tins of powdered milk that were so carefully guarded in the hospital's pharmacy— each about enough for one small child for two weeks—cost just over six dollars apiece. The fifty cents I gave a shoeshine boy outside our hotel was literally more than this dedicated, highly trained physician made each day. Clearly she kept at it out of love for the children, not for the pay.

In our five trucks were enough antibiotics for at least 2,000 patients and almost 20,000 IV kits especially designed for infants dying of dehydration. The physicians had been forced to do surgery on screaming children without anesthesia, and we brought enough to relieve a huge amount of pain. We also had brought 73,000 syringes to replace ones that had been used over and over. The doctors told us that these alone would save the lives of many of their patients. With no new syringes available to them, they had been doing their best to sterilize old ones and reuse them. Despite their efforts, they knew that diseases were sure to be spread at times from one child to the next. However, they had no choice but to take the chance.

Our MCC friends in Amman had even been able to respond to special "shopping lists" for specific medicines needed by particular children, sent from Baghdad by the pediatricians. It became clear that our efforts were going to help save the lives of thousands of small children. Taking that medicine to the hospitals—one big truck to each location—was one of the most joyful, rewarding experiences I have ever had in my life! I watched, sometimes with tears in my eyes, as the doctors themselves excitedly helped us unload tons of this precious cargo for their little patients.

We had included in each load the special medicines or supplies requested by the doctors at a given hospital—more rehydration supplies for those with the most infants dying from diarrhea, lots of Halothane and other anesthesia for those where children were sent for surgery, and so on. In front of the big Mansour Pediatric Hospital in central Baghdad, a doctor spotted the supply of special medication we had brought for one of his patients who was dying from a disease resistant to more common antibiotics. He lifted the package above his head and practically danced in a circle, shouting, "This is exactly what I need to save Ahmed's life!"

Suddenly I found that I needed to walk away for a bit and regain my composure. I went to the steps at the edge of the hospital's parking lot and leaned against a handrail. After all our months of prayer, agonizing over what to do, and lots of hard work, the reward had come. I was overflowing with gratitude to God for allowing me to have such an incredible experience.

Before we left Iraq, we went to the United Nations headquarters in Baghdad and visited with several officials to learn more about their work. These international staff members were unanimous in their frustration with the situation, especially with the pressures from the United States on other U.N. members to make the sanctions still harsher.

"Supposedly we are in this country to bring peace," one of them sputtered. "But we are not cultivating peace here. We are planting the seeds of hatred and violence, of vengeance.

"I know you are here to help with your shipment of medicine," he continued. "But when you return home, you must help Americans understand that the sanctions are mass punishment of innocent people, the children most of all."

We were in the offices of the U.N. Humanitarian Coordinator, with the people responsible for carrying out the so-called Oil for Food program and helping the civilians of Iraq. The director of the program was Denis Halliday, a veteran U.N. official from Ireland. A few months after our visit, he resigned in protest over the sanctions, describing them as a "totally bankrupt concept" that "probably strengthens the leadership and further weakens the people of the country."[2] His successor, Hans von Sponeck of Germany, lasted a little over a year in the same post before resigning in protest as well.

I had been aware all along that most of the other nations of the world were becoming increasingly upset by Americans' apparent lack of empathy for those suffering in Iraq. I had run into this "hardness of heart" myself in dozens of American audiences when I was speaking, even in churches. I had grown up believing that our nation was the great example of generosity and mercy for the downtrodden and the homeless. And I had always thought that most of the world saw our Statue of Liberty as the perfect symbol of America.

But I was learning that the rest of the world viewed us in a very different light. The Soviet Union had come apart only seven years earlier. As the world's sole remaining superpower, the United States was in real danger of changing into something more like the new Roman Empire in the eyes of former friends and admirers. Increasingly, polls were beginning to indicate that these people were becoming afraid of us.

On our last night in Baghdad, I was pondering these matters. I was very much aware that, as wonderful as it had been to help these Iraqi children, I had a huge communications task before me when I got home. Back in the Al Rasheed Hotel, I knelt down beside my bed and prayed for guidance and strength to continue whatever work God had for me to do.

I climbed into bed and tried to sleep, but I kept seeing the faces of the kids who I knew were suffering all over Baghdad and beyond. The image came to me of another great disaster about which all students knew, the sinking of the *Titanic* in 1912. It suddenly seemed strange to me that we would make so much of a tragedy that had taken the lives of 1,500 people almost a century earlier—and not grasp that a disaster of far greater magnitude was taking place now in Iraq. Indeed, it was as if *almost once a week* another *Titanic* was being filled with small children, towed out into the ocean, and sunk, with the loss of every little passenger on the ship!

Then it occurred to me in my sleeplessness that one of the key people in the middle of this tragedy, UNSCOM director Richard Butler, was probably down the hall somewhere right there in the Al Rasheed Hotel. I decided that he should know that we had been praying for him as the news media in the U.S. and around the world reported the work of his international team of weapons investigators. I could hardly imagine the tremendous pressures he must have felt every day.

I climbed out of bed and wrote a letter to Butler. I told him about our delivery of medicine to the hospitals without permission from the U.S. government. "I want you to know of our prayers that God will guide you during this time of great difficulty for all peacemakers.... May God truly give you love, wisdom, and courage." I enclosed a copy of the Jubilee Partners newsletter that had called specifically for prayer for him.

I dressed and took the letter down to the front desk of the hotel. "Please pass this letter to Richard Butler," I requested of the startled concierge. He hesitated, and then agreed to do so. After breakfast the next morning, I was checking out of the hotel and preparing for the long drive back to Amman. "Oh, excuse me, Mr. Mosley, but I have a letter for you," said the man behind the counter.

When I opened the envelope, I was amazed to find an immediate response from Richard Butler. It reminded me that I had heard from a friend who had met him that Butler is a very sincere Christian. His letter certainly indicated that. "I was very touched by your note," he began. Then he wrote that he shared my concern for the children of Iraq. Acknowledging the beginning of Lent, he wrote, "I was struck when reading this morning by the fact that, in the cycle of the church we are also beginning, today, the approach to the greatest mystery... the great Jubilee." After suggesting that I read what he had just read—Isaiah 10—he concluded, "God bless you and your work. Sincerely, Richard Butler."

I opened my briefcase and found the Scripture in my Bible. What I read—especially under these dramatic circumstances— made me feel almost as though I was hearing the words directly from Isaiah himself:

> Shame on you! you who make unjust laws
> and publish burdensome decrees,
> depriving the poor of justice,
> robbing the weakest of my people of their rights,
> despoiling the widow and plundering the orphan.
> What will you do when called to account,

when ruin from afar confronts you?
To whom will you flee for help
and where will you leave your children,
so that they do not cower before the [jailer]
or fall by the executioner's hand?
For all this his anger has not turned back,
and his hand is stretched out still. (verses 1-4, NEB)

I knew that I had just been given an answer to my prayer beside the bed the night before. "His hand is stretched out still"—but for how long? I felt an urgent need to take some of the insights I had gained in Iraq back home and share them with my American brothers and sisters, in our churches or wherever else I could find people who would listen.

We set out back across the desert with Samir at the wheel of his Suburban. This time he was more rested, so we could relax a little and get some sleep as we hurtled along through the night. Shortly after daybreak, however, our trip almost came to a sudden, permanent end.

In 1998 Jordan was still buying a huge amount of oil from Iraq each year. It was carried across the desert in big tanker trucks, some of which were driven by people who were probably better suited for some other profession. On the Iraqi side, Saddam had built a divided highway equal to anything in Europe or North America. West of the border, however, the Jordanian section of the highway narrowed to two lanes, with only a thin shoulder between the traffic and endless stretches of stones and boulders scattered across sand.

Having crossed into Jordan, but still driving at racetrack speed, Samir was approaching the crest of a steep hill when suddenly we found ourselves facing two oncoming tankers, one of them filling our lane as it came straight toward us! Samir barely managed to swing the wheel to the right and throw us off the highway as the two trucks flashed by us side by side. Against all odds, he managed to fishtail the car along through the loose stones and back onto the highway without flipping over, still moving at very high speed.

Apparently God had more work for us to do back in North America!

As soon as we got home, I set out on more speaking trips. I wanted to help persuade as many people as possible to join us in a campaign of compassion against the evil that was killing so many children in Iraq and—as the U.N. official had put it— "planting the seeds of hatred and violence, of vengeance."

The response from the audiences and our Jubilee supporters continued to be strong. It was so good, in fact, that we soon made plans for another shipment of medicine to the Iraqi hospitals. I invited a long-time friend, Ladon Sheats, to lead the next delegation. He quickly said yes, and soon he had recruited three other people to go with him. By the time they were ready to go in September, we had raised another $70,000 for medicine.

In another adventure-filled trip, the four of them delivered seven or eight more truckloads of medicine to the pediatric hospitals. Maybe we couldn't stop the horrible suffering completely, but we had delivered enough medicine in one year to save the lives of many children. It was as though we had managed to keep that *Titanic* in port, not just once but at least four or five times— and escort all the children back to shore.

There seems to be a law, however, that just when we think we have won a great victory—look out! Trouble is on the way. This was to be no exception.

I was on the road for much of the time over the next several months, urging people in churches and on college campuses to inform themselves about Iraq and then to help persuade our leaders to change our policies in the Middle East. I returned home from one of these trips in mid-January 1999, and found a letter from the Department of the Treasury, Office of Foreign Assets Control (OFAC). It was from the head of OFAC's Enforcement Division:

Recent newspaper articles reported that you recently traveled to Iraq as part of a delegation from Jubilee Partners to deliver medicine in Iraq that was purchased in Jordan. If the transactions were accurately reported, they may constitute violations of the Regulations.

No specific license was issued to you.... You should be aware that penalties for individuals violating the Regulations range up to $275,000 per count for each civil violation, and up to $1,000,000 and/or 12 years in prison for each criminal violation.

They had my attention. I kept reading. The letter stated that I had twenty business days to answer in writing a list of questions about our trip to Iraq. They especially wanted to know exactly why we had gone and what we had taken with us. I answered the letter as fully and honestly as I could. More questions came, and I sent more answers.

This process continued for almost two years. Finally, I received notice that I was being fined $30,000 by OFAC. I responded that I was ready to go to prison if necessary, but that I would not pay a cent as a penalty for breaking a law that was wrong in the first place. I wrote to the director of OFAC on December 28, 2000:

I took the medicine to the Iraqi children after many months of praying and thinking about the matter and seeking the advice of friends. I believed then—and I believe even more strongly now—that it is wrong for us to carry out a program of sanctions against the most innocent people in all of Iraq, children who were born years after the Gulf War and who have utterly no power to influence their dictator. I believe that we should have sanctions against Saddam Hussein, sanctions genuinely designed and executed in such a way that they address his *military* strength. Instead, we have sanctions that are carried out in such a way that they actually *strengthen* him politically and make us look like cruel monsters at worst or careless and clumsy violators of basic human rights at best.

This is not only politically counterproductive, it is morally wrong. It is also incredibly shortsighted. Through this and other similar displays of apparent disregard for innocent Arab children, we are recruiting young people of the region into the ranks of violent people like Osama bin Laden more effectively than he ever could without our help. How can we not expect this to escalate the likelihood of violence between us?

I was writing nine months before the planes hit the World Trade Center and the Pentagon, but already I could see glimpses of the inevitable result of our misguided policy. My letter continued:

I am fully aware that, at best, my actions probably look naïve to you. Undoubtedly they are, to some extent at least, even though I can point to a lifetime of study and direct experience in international and cross-cultural situations.

I believe, however, that there is another kind of naïveté which permeates a situation of this type, an officially acceptable naïveté assumed by our policy makers and enforcers. Almost *none* of the top members of our government have gone to the Iraqi pediatric hospitals as I have, where they would come face-to-face with the small children who are dying at the documented rate of several hundred per day. I am sure you are aware of the senior U.N. officials who resigned in protest against this policy, precisely because they *had* seen its effects at first hand. I don't believe those U.N. officials were somehow morally superior to most of the men and women who make up our government; I believe the difference is that their circumstances brought them into direct contact with a situation about which our own leaders have chosen to remain, in a very real sense, officially naïve.

As a Christian, I try to understand and to follow—though very imperfectly at best—the model and teachings of Jesus Christ in such matters. I believe that the best in Christianity (as well as in other religions) always calls on us to be compassionate peacemakers in a world where that sometimes appears to others to be naïve.

Sincerely,

Don Mosley

Carolyn and I didn't know what to expect next. Certainly one strong possibility was that I would be put in prison. George W. Bush was the brand-new president-elect. Not sure what to expect of his administration, we lived each day knowing that we could be separated for a long time if the U.S. government decided to jail me. But we reminded each other frequently that the whole matter was in God's hands, not ours.

Some weeks later, we got a telephone call from the OFAC office. A rather soft-spoken man said, "Mr. Mosley, we have been reconsidering your case. Given the humanitarian nature of your actions in Iraq, we are prepared to offer you a reduction in the penalty you must pay. We have decided to fine you only one-fourth as much as we said initially—that is, seven thousand five hundred dollars."

Trying my best not to sound triumphant, I responded that I appreciated their consideration but that I was still firmly convinced I should not pay a cent. It was a matter of principle for me. To pay any fine at all would amount to a concession that the law was somehow legitimate. The man with the gentle voice assured me that I would be hearing from them again soon and hung up.

I did not hear from OFAC again, at least not directly. Instead, I got several threatening calls from commercial bill collectors hired by OFAC. Eventually, in a case similar to mine in Seattle, a federal judge slapped the hands of government officials for resorting to such tactics, and even the calls came to a stop for me. I was free to turn my attention to another group of young people who were bringing their unique and disturbing needs to the doorstep of Jubilee.

CHAPTER FIVE

I'm Not Lost from God

T ry to imagine a catastrophe that drives thousands of small children out across the deserts of Arizona and New Mexico. Imagine more than 20,000 of them—most six, eight, ten years old—wandering for years, covering a thousand miles, some preyed upon by wild animals, others hunted down and killed by soldiers. Picture a huge camp in which the half who survive live in a city of children, huddled in brush and mud shelters they built themselves to escape the scorching heat of the desert sun.

This is not the plot of a Hollywood horror film. Such a cataclysm happened, not in the southwestern United States, but in northeastern Africa. Many of its survivors are still in a United Nations camp today, more than two decades later. In the wilderness of northwestern Kenya, visited by dust storms and drought, plagued by malnutrition and malaria, the Kakuma camp has been home to 70,000 refugees from several African nations. The Lost Boys of Sudan have been its most renowned residents.

Among the Dinkas and other southern tribes, it is the custom for sons to spend much of their time tending cattle out in the bush while their parents and sisters remain at home. So it was that in 1987, countless boys watched in horror from a distance as planes swooped down and dropped bombs on their villages in southern

Sudan. In many cases, northern Sudanese troops then laid siege, shooting the surviving men and enslaving women and girls.

The attacks wiped out one village after another and orphaned thousands of young boys. Word spread among them that they could find safety in neighboring Ethiopia, already a haven for the Sudan People's Liberation Army (SPLA). It is likely that the SPLA promoted this movement of the boys toward Ethiopia so that the rebel soldiers could recruit or kidnap them into their ranks and send them back into Sudan to fight the northern Sudanese troops.

Thousands of boys headed through wilderness toward the Gilo River on the border, often with hostile soldiers in pursuit. Terrified, the children had to hide like wild animals to survive. After they arrived in Ethiopia, a change in that country's government closed the door on them, and they were forced back to Sudan. As they tried to recross the river, many drowned, some were killed by crocodiles, and others were shot by Ethiopian soldiers.

Those who survived were forced a few months later by northern Sudanese soldiers to flee once more for their lives. This time they headed south to Kenya. After many more hardships, the weak, exhausted, half-starved children were allowed to settle in the Kakuma camp. Kakuma is Swahili for "nowhere."

Sudan is the largest country in Africa, equal in size to the United States east of the Mississippi River. Thirty million people are scattered over its considerable area. The country's long civil war has been one of the bloodiest conflicts since World War II, claiming the lives of 2 million people and displacing more than twice that many.

As in most wars, the conflict has multiple causes, with religion and race being major contributing factors. More than two-thirds of the Sudanese are Sunni Muslims. Most of the people in northern Sudan are light-skinned Muslim Arabs, while those in the south and west are predominantly dark-skinned Africans. Between 1 and 2 million southern Sudanese are Christians, but several times that many practice indigenous religions.

The civil war is not as simple as a conflict between Muslims and Christians, as some have characterized it. It is true that the present national leaders in Khartoum are Islamic fundamentalists, led by President Omar al-Bashir, who has the distinction of being the first sitting head of state ever to be formally charged with genocide by the prosecutor of the International Criminal Court. But in recent years, the conflict in Sudan has shifted largely from the southern to the western part of the country, where the dark-skinned Muslims of Darfur are suffering from the brutality of the Khartoum government. Omar al-Bashir has carried out his murderous policies against Muslims as well as Christians.

In 1999, U.S. authorities agreed to resettle 3,600 of the Lost Boys as political refugees in the United States. Early in 2001, we welcomed our first two to Jubilee. One turned out not to be a "lost boy" at all, but a teenage girl! Sarah Solomon arrived with her older brother, Emmanuel. She was only six years old when the two of them had been forced to begin their thousand-mile struggle for survival.

Emmanuel had distinguished himself as such a bright and diligent student that he was one of a few young refugees chosen for specialized education in Kenya. These refugees then served as teachers to the other youth at Kakuma. Emmanuel spent his first paycheck on a pretty dress for his little sister. Twice he declined college scholarships in other countries, because accepting them would have required him to leave Sarah behind. For us at Jubilee, this incredible young pair of sibling survivors were the perfect introduction to some of the most amazing and inspiring refugees in the world.

Seventeen more Lost Boys arrived in the spring of 2001. Most were no longer boys, but young men, though their exact ages and birth dates were lost in their exodus from Sudan. U.S. immigration officials guessed at their ages and assigned January 1 as their universal birthday. Their stories are among the most dramatic we've ever heard.

"At night we slept in trees for safety," Matiop Kech Deng told our wide-eyed Jubilee children about his first terrifying nights in the wilderness. "One time I went up first while my friend waited. Just after I found a place to sleep, I looked down and saw that a lion had killed my friend and was eating him."

Abraham Yel Nhial had become a Christian during his brief stay in Ethiopia. Then, while still a teenager himself, he had begun to serve as a pastor to hundreds of other young Sudanese. When a team of reporters from the news show *60 Minutes* appeared in Kenya to film an episode about the Lost Boys, they were so impressed with Abraham's leadership and character that they made him a central figure in their report to the American people. They showed him leading worship in the makeshift Kakuma church, discovering his name on the bulletin board as one of those chosen for resettlement in the United States, and saying good-bye to his many friends at the camp as he prepared to depart.

When a few of us from Jubilee went to the Atlanta airport to meet Abraham and the rest of the group, there at the gate was the *60 Minutes* film crew, covering the next stage of this unfolding human drama. Over the next few days we became well acquainted with the crew members as they worked on their story at Jubilee. The cameras zoomed in as the young men were introduced to one marvel after another: refrigerators, cooking ranges, electric lights, flush toilets, and hot water right out of the tap.

Among the most astonishing realities to the young Sudanese was the quantity and variety of food available here. As they stared at the food that was waiting for them on their arrival, the only things they recognized were salt and bananas. Fruit was a rare treat back in the refugee camp.

"We only ate once a day at Kakuma," said one, as the others nodded. "There were hard times when we had no food at all for a week at a time." Their lanky frames confirmed reports that for years they had been surviving on nothing more than a bit of wheat or corn flour and about a cup of lentils per month.

The young men were eager learners. Cooking classes included new skills such as thawing frozen foods, steaming rice, and dealing with a bewildering array of wrappers and containers. "That is a wonderful machine," observed one about a can opener.

The gulf between their experiences and ours was sometimes greater than we could readily grasp. One evening, some of us from Jubilee were telling four of the Sudanese men about having just spent several days backpacking on the Appalachian Trail, adding that two of our community visitors had once hiked the trail's entire 2,100 miles. These veterans of years in the wilderness without camping equipment looked baffled. Finally one of them asked quietly, "Why?"

We were most touched by these young men's care for one another and the extraordinary bond that existed among them, forged in unspeakable hardship. "You have to have a group," Matiop explained. "You cannot be alone and survive. Without a group, you sit by yourself and think about the past and all the terrible things that have happened. You cannot live alone like that. A group keeps you talking, laughing, living in the present."

The plight of the Lost Boys had come to my attention at least a year before the first ones arrived among us. In October 1999, I had given a talk at Brevard College in western North Carolina. I spoke about Jubliee's peacemaking efforts in the Middle East, and I stressed how important it is that Christians and Muslims begin to understand each other better.

As soon as I ended my talk, a man from the audience approached and thanked me vigorously. "My name is Gasim Abdulkarim," he said. "My wife and I are Muslims from Sudan, but we live right here in Brevard with our children. What you have said is so important and so true. You cannot imagine how glad I am to hear you say it!"

Carolyn and I were so impressed with Gasim and his wife, Nawal, that we soon returned to Brevard and visited their home. We learned that Gasim had worked in two different U.S. embassies and that he had made such a favorable impression on his American supervisors that he was granted permission to move to the United States with his family. We soon became very fond of all of them.

So it was not a total surprise when we got a call from Gasim in June 2001, saying that he and Nawal would like to come to Jubilee for a visit with our young Sudanese refugees. "But, Gasim," I answered, "I really don't know how these young guys from southern Sudan will respond to Muslim visitors from Khartoum. I would try to assure them that you are my friends, but..."

"Don, please don't worry about it at all," he responded. "I am very sympathetic with these Lost Boys who have suffered so much, and I am eager to tell them that personally. I want them to meet my whole family and get to know us as fellow human beings from Sudan. Don't worry. I know it will go all right."

And indeed it did! There were a few awkward moments after I introduced Gasim's family and the young men to one another. But within minutes, our Muslim guests were sitting at a picnic table at the Jubilee Welcome Center, surrounded by a crowd of fascinated Lost Boys. The eagerness of all of them to reach out to one another was obvious.

As was usually the case, Abraham served as the chief spokesman for the young men, but the others frequently shared in the lively conversation. Something rare and beautiful was taking place. Gasim and Nawal made clear that they deeply regretted what had happened to these young men and their families. Their sincerity was unmistakable. After a couple of hours with the entire group, I ushered Gasim and Abraham to the Jubilee dining room where they could continue their discussion with more privacy. I sensed that a bond of trust was beginning to develop between them.

"Abraham," said Gasim, "you will always be welcome in my home if you ever get a chance to visit."

"I know that I would be treated like one of your own family," responded Abraham.

What came next was one of the most dramatic surprises I have ever experienced. Gasim said, "You know, of course, who was Prime Minister of Sudan when your village was bombed—Sadiq al-Mahdi."

"Of course," Abraham nodded. "How could I ever forget that?"

Gasim took a deep breath and continued. "Well, Sadiq is my cousin! Actually he is my second cousin. Both of us are great-grandsons of Muhammad Ahmed al Mahdi." Even I knew whom he referred to—the man who had defeated the British general Charles George Gordon in 1885. I immediately thought back to the old movie Khartoum, with Lawrence Olivier's Mahdi over-powering Charlton Heston's Gordon.

Gasim pushed ahead. "Abraham, it happens that Sadiq is in Washington at this very moment, talking to U.S. officials about how to help end the war in Sudan. I believe he would be willing to meet with us and hear you tell of your experiences. Would you be willing to talk to him if I could arrange a meeting?"

Abraham agreed at once. I offered immediately to provide the transportation and a place to stay in Washington. Within hours, Gasim confirmed that Sadiq al-Mahdi had a strong interest in meeting personally with Abraham, to hear for himself about the suffering of the Lost Boys and their communities.

Five days later, on June 15, 2001, we were face-to-face with the man who, though not in full control of the situation in 1987, nevertheless had presided over the slaughter of thousands of Dinkas and other southern Sudanese people and shared responsibility for years of suffering by the surviving children. Sadiq al-Mahdi, in his mid-60s, was a sophisticated and articulate graduate of Oxford University. He sat almost directly in front of me in an armchair, opposite the couch on which the others sat. Abraham was on my right, with Gasim just beyond him.

As though he had been preparing for this meeting through those long years in the desert, Abraham spoke clearly and forcefully about the suffering of his people. As he described one terrible event after another, Sadiq listened intently. He was leaning forward slightly, the muscles of his face reflecting his growing emotions. He kept both hands cupped over the upper end of a carved walking stick between his knees. Not once did he interrupt or dispute Abraham's narrative.

Then came the most extraordinary moment in this amazing sequence of events. Abraham, the poised young Christian pastor of the Lost Boys, astonished Sadiq al-Mahdi by insisting that he had no desire for revenge. Instead, he said he prayed for reconciliation between the north and the south. He yearned for the chance to work together with all the people of Sudan for a better future. "The children of Sudan must never again know suffering like we have endured," concluded Abraham. "We must work together to guarantee that."

Sadiq suddenly stood to his feet and exclaimed, "You should be known not as the Lost Boys but as the 'peace boys.' And to think—we have been led to believe that the United States brought thousands of you to this country to train you as a fighting force for military action in Sudan!" He paused and then said, "Abraham, I am convinced that you are telling me the truth about your desire for peace in Sudan. But are you sure that your feelings are shared widely by the other Lost Boys?"

"Yes. I know my people. I am sure of it," Abraham said.

Gasim then showed Sadiq a chilling photograph, which had just been awarded a Pulitzer Prize. It was of a starving, southern Sudanese little girl, so weak that she could barely lift her head. A huge vulture was perched nearby, watching hungrily for a chance to devour her when she died. I was sitting so close to Sadiq that I could have touched his face with my hand—and he looked like a man about to break into tears. Something incredible was happening in that room.

Finally Sadiq said, "Abraham, I have a favor to ask of you. I want you to get in touch with as many of the other Lost Boys as you can, to be sure they really agree with what you have told me. If they do, I will go back to Sudan and personally call for a formal apology to the people of southern Sudan. We must make it possible for you Lost Boys to come back and join in the reconstruction of Sudan."

As we left Sadiq's hotel, I told Abraham that I wanted him to see another Abraham—this one a president of whom most of us in the United States are quite proud. I drove him and Gasim to the Lincoln Memorial. Standing beside the statue of the great statesman, I talked about racism and slavery in America. I described the great 1963 March on Washington that converged at the monument, and the "I Have a Dream" speech delivered there by Dr. Martin Luther King. With curious tourists glancing or staring at us, I stood between Abraham and Gasim as Gasim read Lincoln's Gettysburg Address aloud from its inscription on the memorial's wall.

We had just crossed the Potomac on our way home when Gasim turned to Abraham and offered him the use of his cell phone to begin calling other Lost Boys to see how they might react to what had happened. Abraham had never used a cell phone, but over the next five hours he became an expert. He had a small book filled with telephone numbers. Hour after hour he called one young man after another and described the incredible meeting we had just shared with Sadiq al-Mahdi. Our meeting had been in English, but late that evening as Abraham talked on the phone, Gasim told me admiringly, "This guy has been using at least four other languages to report to the others. What a communicator!"

We reached Gasim's home in North Carolina about midnight. As Abraham finished the last of his many conversations, we asked him eagerly, "Well, what about it? Did they agree with the statement you made to Sadiq?"

"Yes," he smiled, as he returned the cell phone to Gasim. "Every single one of them agreed!"

It was three o'clock in the morning when Abraham and I reached Jubilee. After a very brief sleep, he and I began working together to get his statement into a form for distribution. Within a couple of days, Abraham was satisfied with it. We began to send it out by fax, email, and letter to all the Lost Boys we could find around the country, inviting them to add their signatures to the statement:

Lost Boys' Call for Peace

We are called the "Lost Boys of Sudan," but we are lost only from our parents, not from God. Our families and villages have been destroyed by war. We have walked a thousand miles (1,600 km) in Sudan, Ethiopia, and Kenya. For fourteen years we have suffered terrible hardships, such that at least half of our original number have died. Despite this our faith is still strong. But those of us who have survived this long suffering believe that God is now giving us an opportunity to work for the good of the people of our country.

Almost four thousand of us are coming to the United States this year as refugees. The story is spreading in Sudan that we are preparing to return someday as soldiers, to fight against those who have destroyed our families. That is not true, because there has already been too much killing, too much suffering in our country.

Our profound hope is that a lasting peace agreement will be quickly reached in our country. We earnestly desire peace, not revenge. We want no more weapons killing any of our Sudanese brothers and sisters, from the north of Sudan or from the south of Sudan. All of us were created by one God, and it is time for us to forgive and embrace each other.

We declare to our brothers and sisters in all parts of Sudan, as well as those who wait as refugees in Kenya and other places—we will not abandon you! We will build friendship between our people and the people of the United States. We will use our opportunity to gain education and resources and to return to Sudan as soon as possible. We have a great dream for the future of our country. We want to work together with all Sudanese to rebuild our houses, schools, and hospitals. We want to raise enough food so that hunger will end. We want all of our younger brothers and sisters in all parts of Sudan to be able to live together in peace, never again suffering what we have endured.

We pray to God that all Sudanese people will join in this great work for a future in peace.

Less than a week after our meeting with Sadiq al-Mahdi, I drove our Jubilee bus with nearly thirty Lost Boys to Atlanta. Jimmy and Rosalynn Carter and their staff wanted to meet these outstanding young men. The Carter Center had an office in Khartoum and a staff of experts working hard to help bring about a peace settlement in Sudan.

The day went beautifully. The Carters and their center's associate director of conflict resolution, Tom Crick, spent a couple of hours with the Lost Boys. Staff members who had returned from East Africa only a couple of days earlier briefed them on the state of Sudanese peace negotiations. Abraham and the others asked questions and added their own observations. Meanwhile, the *60 Minutes* film crew took it all in for their report to be broadcast in the latter half of September.

As usual, the earnest young men charmed everyone they met. Abraham was a young Christian leader with no illusions about what violence had already cost his people. More than that, he was incredulous that, of all people, the followers of Jesus would advocate still more violence. Puzzled, he shook his head and exclaimed, "I was ordained as a pastor of the Gospel of Jesus Christ. Then how can I choose to *kill* my enemy?"

President Carter was deeply impressed with Abraham and the others. When he read the Lost Boys' Call for Peace and heard the story of our meeting with Sadiq al-Mahdi, he became very excited. "Please let me know when you are ready to issue the statement formally, and I will be happy to help promulgate it to heads of state all over Africa," he said. We assured him that we would welcome his help.

A lot of work was required to find addresses for the Lost Boys scattered all over the country, to get the Call for Peace to them, and then to record the signatures of those who signed it. Some sent word that they agreed fully with the statement but were afraid to attach their names to it because they weren't sure what impact it might have on the safety of friends or family back in Sudan. Nevertheless, by the end of that summer of 2001, 155 of them had signed the statement. More signatures were coming every day as it was copied and passed along.

Those weeks were extremely exciting for me. I was thrilled to be in the middle of such an extraordinary movement of peace-making and reconciliation, to be helping this wave of goodwill build higher and higher. I had little doubt that it would soon sweep over the evil that had cost so many lives in the world's bloodiest civil war in half a century.

Abraham felt that the appropriate way to release the Lost Boys' Call for Peace was first to publish it in the Jubilee Partners newsletter, sent to our mailing list of almost 12,000 names. We alerted several journalist friends and others in key places that we would fax or email copies in English and Arabic to them imme-diately after the newsletter went to the post office. President Carter would simultaneously convey it to appropriate heads of state.

Our printer in Athens, Georgia, rushed copies of the newsletter out to us as soon as they were off the press. We recruited every-one we could find to help address the thousands of copies and pre-pare them for mailing. Finally the happy day came. I loaded several hundred pounds of newsletters into our van and delivered them to the post office in Comer as soon as it opened its doors. It was Monday morning, September 10, 2001.

With the newsletter finally on its way, I turned my attention to preparations for a trip to Africa and the Middle East. Among other objectives, Carolyn and I had been feeling for some time that we should go to Lebanon and Jordan to try to help establish Habitat for Humanity programs there. I called our travel agent and made an appointment for the next morning.

Our work in her office on the complicated itinerary was interrupted by a commotion out in the lobby of the agency. Staff members were gathering excitedly around a small television set. We decided to suspend our work for a few minutes and find out what was going on.

The second airliner had just crashed into the South Tower of the World Trade Center. When a plane hit the Pentagon a few minutes later, it was clear that a coordinated attack was under way. The immediate assumption among the small cluster of people in the travel agency was that it had been launched by Middle Eastern terrorists. As I gathered my papers and prepared to leave, our travel agent said, "Well, I guess that changes your plans about a trip to the Middle East, doesn't it?"

"Not necessarily," I answered. "In fact, it may be more important than ever now."

I wish I could honestly say that as I left the travel agency I was calmly confident God was fully in control of whatever was going on, and that the euphoria I had been feeling the day before would continue without interruption. The truth is, of course, that I was feeling shaken and confused. I didn't know why these things were happening. But I had a steady conviction that we should trust God and move ahead with whatever actions we could take to try to overcome this great evil with good.

The Lost Boys' Call for Peace took a direct hit from the 9/11 attacks. A gang of young men beat one of the Lost Boys in Atlanta, shouting, "Why did you attack America?" They then smashed the windows in his apartment, clearly unaware of the tragic irony of their actions. They could hardly have found in all the city a less appropriate target for their outrage. All over the United States, similar outbursts of violence erupted against innocent people who somehow seemed to represent a threat. In particular, the Muslim community in the United States was under attack, as mosque after mosque was threatened or defaced in various ways.

Abraham called me from Atlanta after a few days. "Don, it is very painful to say this," he said, "but we must not publicize our Call for Peace. Our people are afraid to continue with it right now. We don't know what the effect might be, and we are already receiving many threats." It was clear that the Lost Boys were feeling pursued by horrors that they had thought were forever behind them.

I could not disagree with their decision, of course. We quickly prepared a letter and sent it to all the people on our mailing list, retracting the Call for Peace and explaining that the Lost Boys were "people who understand well from personal experience how it feels to be victims of terrorists and hatred. Ironically, they are now having to guard against attacks from some people in the United States who express their own anger by lashing out against anyone different from themselves."

The growing fear and distrust between Christians and Muslims is the tragic and continuing fallout from the 9/11 attacks. More than 2 billion people on our planet identify themselves as Christians, and about 1.2 billion as Muslims. Together, these followers of the world's two largest monotheistic religions, claiming a common parentage through the patriarch Abraham, make up more than half of the human race: 33 percent and 20 percent respectively. It happens that the 33 percent are the biggest consumers of the shrinking oil reserves owned mostly by the 20 percent.

In 2005 I was in Cairo, Egypt, on Habitat for Humanity business. There I had a long, stimulating conversation with a leading Egyptian intellectual, Nabil Abdel-Fattah. A lawyer and a prolific writer, Nabil is also a leader in the Al-Ahram Centre for Political and Strategic Studies. He writes regularly in *Al-Ahram,* one of the most important newspapers in the Middle East.

Nabil and I were discussing the reactions both in the United States and in the Middle East to the September 11 attacks on the World Trade Center and the Pentagon. Both of us were deeply concerned about the way political leaders in both parts of the world made use of public fears to increase their own power. Nabil, as an Egyptian journalist, is especially conscious of the ability of the news media to shape the way we see each other.

When Nabil and I talked, Robert W. McChesney's important book *The Problem of the Media* had just been published. He made a very similar criticism of U.S. journalism. McChesney described two of its greatest shortcomings as "sensationalism" and "avoidance of contextualization." He then claimed that "far from being politically neutral, journalism smuggles in values conducive to the commercial aims of owners and advertisers and to the political aims of big business." He added, "Arguably the weakest feature of U.S. professional journalism has been its coverage of the nation's role in the world, especially when military action is involved."[1]

In Cairo, Nabil said, "There is nothing more dangerous right now than the distortion of truth, whether by deliberate intent or not. The most important challenge we face—if we would be peacemakers in this dangerous world—is to work against the negative stereotypes that are spreading and dominating on both sides these days. I travel in the U.S. and like the American people very much. But when I come home to Egypt, I am very disturbed by the negative images I see, not only in our media but also in the violence and immorality of your Hollywood movies and television programs. I see a very similar distortion [about us] when I am in America."

Such a climate helped make Samuel P. Huntington's *The Clash of Civilizations and the Remaking of World Order* a *New York Times* bestseller. Head of Harvard University's Academy for

International and Area Studies, Huntington was a political scientist with a huge amount of influence on our top policy makers.

Huntington's book chronicles the history of national alliances through recent centuries, the wars between those alliances, and the present "multipolar *and* multicivilizational" character of the world. Huntington argues that "avoidance of a global war of civilizations depends on world leaders accepting and cooperating to maintain the multicivilizational character of global politics."[2] Later he observes that "conflicts between the West and Islam...focus less on territory than on broader intercivilizational issues such as weapons proliferation, human rights and democracy, control of oil, migration, Islamist terrorism, and Western intervention."[3]

There is much in Huntington's book that contradicts my own observations in the Middle East, and a pervasive sense of hopelessness that runs counter to my faith. But one of his assertions resonates strongly with what I have seen there. He states that the biggest problem for most Muslims is not with Christianity itself, but with the people of the West who appear to them not to adhere to any religion at all. "In Muslim eyes Western secularism, irreligiosity, and hence immorality" are the real problems. "In the Cold War the West labeled its opponent 'godless communism'; in the post-Cold War conflict of civilizations Muslims see their opponent as 'the godless West.' "[4]

Yousry Makar agrees, and he is in a far better position to judge such things than I am. Yousry is the national director of Habitat for Humanity in Egypt. He was born in the heart of Cairo, the son of one of the most prominent Presbyterian pastors in Egypt. As we have traveled together on speaking trips from coast to coast in the United States and worked together repeatedly in Egypt, Yousry has become like an Egyptian brother to me.

Responding specifically to Huntington's book, Yousry said, "The alternative to 'clashing' is dialogue. Clashing never solves any problem. We each have to find ways to work together, to speak and understand the language of the person on the other side, to show respect and compassion for each other. For instance, we do not discriminate between Muslims and Christians in the distribution of Habitat houses. We arrange constantly for Muslims and Christians to help each other build those houses. We even provide chances for foreign volunteers to work with the Egyptian Muslims and Christians."

Yousry is an energetic Christian engineer, fluent in English, deeply devoted to serving the people of Egypt as a demonstration of his Christian commitment. Carolyn and I like very much the way he talks about his personal goal of "showing Egyptians a different face of Jesus" by building a quarter of a million homes for people who are living in extremely poor conditions. And Yousry is not just talk; he is a man of action.

In just a few short years he has led his team from building 300 houses a year to more than 2,000 a year, making the Habitat program in Egypt one of the most vigorous in the world. As I write this book, they are building or renovating the 15,000th house along the Nile River! Though that's not yet a quarter of a million, the rate of construction is increasing exponentially. Just give Yousry a little more time.

For years I have used the work of Habitat in Egypt as an illustration of how to be real peacemakers in this world. Many times I have pointed out that a single Tomahawk cruise missile costs some $840,000 to build, and undoubtedly many more thousands to deploy and eventually use against an enemy target. It's good for a single big bang—one time only. Sometimes missiles miss their intended target altogether. Frequently they kill innocent people, including children. I know, because I have gone to some of those targets soon afterward and talked to the survivors. Even if the intended targets are hit, one result that is virtually guaranteed is that bitterness will have been deepened and new recruits attracted into the opposition. Violence always sets the stage for still more violence.

By contrast, spending that same amount of money—the cost of building and using a single cruise missile—for houses along the Nile River would provide comfortable new living quarters for close to 4,000 people. In the process, thousands of others participate in an exciting process that transforms the way they think about each other and about themselves. When the Habitat homeowners pay off their loans, the money is recycled to build still more homes for thousands of their neighbors—year after year.

How on earth can any sane person doubt which use of that million dollars actually does more to promote peace and justice in this world? What has possessed us that we are so out of touch with reality? Who is truly "naïve" about the future?

In 2007, within the space of a few weeks, at least half a dozen people—including my old friend, Millard Fuller—contacted me and urged me to read an exciting book they had discovered. It was another *New York Times* bestseller, *Three Cups of Tea*. When I started reading it, I was so excited by the book that I could hardly put it down to eat. It tells the wonderful story of Greg Mortenson's relentless campaign on behalf of the children—especially the girls—of northern Pakistan and eastern Afghanistan. Through his efforts, dozens of schools have been built and as many as 20,000 children are getting a chance at an education—most of them in an area described by U.S. officials as "the most dangerous place for American nationals on Earth."

Mortenson shuttles back and forth between overseeing this work and speaking to audiences all over the United States. I shouted out loud when, near the end of the book, I read a quote from his speech to a group of high officials in the Pentagon:

> "I'm no military expert...and these figures might not be exactly right. But as best as I can tell, we've launched 114 Tomahawk cruise missiles into Afghanistan so far. Now take the cost of one of those missiles tipped with a Raytheon guid-

ance system, which I think is about $840,000. For that much money, you could build dozens of schools that could provide tens of thousands of students with a balanced nonextremist education over the course of a generation. Which do you think will make us more secure?"[5]

Five days after the 9/11 attacks, Jubilee hosted a picnic in a park near the center of Atlanta. That Sunday afternoon, about 200 Lost Boys, former Jubilee refugees, and other friends gathered to celebrate their friendship and love for one another despite the madness that threatened to destroy us all. Jubilee's Jennifer Drago, small in stature but huge in spirit, spoke to the crowd.

"God bless America," she proclaimed. "And Afghanistan, and Sudan, and Bosnia, and the Congo, and Rwanda, and..." She continued on through the long list of nations represented in the crowd. People smiled as their countries of origin were named, even though most had been driven out of them by war. Each of them knew that there was still much for God to love and bless in their homelands.

One of those present in the crowd was Mana Demaj, the Bosnian Muslim nurse who had served others in Sarajevo so heroically before coming through Jubilee with her son in the mid-1990s. A few weeks after 9/11, Mana wrote a beautiful letter to us:

> Dear Jubilee Partners,
> I just want to say that I do not have words to describe how sorry I am for those people who died in the buildings and for the suffering of those in the airplane before they died. I want you to know that I have empathy for the people who are left behind fatherless, childless, widowed, etc. I am feeling the pain for the fourth time in my life and it really hurts.
> Please do not confuse Islam with those terrorists who caused this evil event, as I did not confuse Serbian and Croatian Christianity with the killing, massacring, and genocide in Bosnia from 1992 to 1995. The word Islam means Peace...

I am writing to you because you mean so much to me since the day I entered in this country. You are my friends, and I care about you. You taught me a lesson, to not hate and forgive those who caused pain in me. It was hard, but as the time went by, I did forgive.

Now, I as a refugee have a message for you. Please do not change no matter what happens, be a good Christian as you have always been. I remind you: do not hate, forgive.

God bless you all,

Mana Demaj

Soon after Mana's letter arrived, we received another humbling communication from a different Muslim friend, Gasim Abdulkarim. Gasim said that he had just been told by relatives back in Sudan that, even without the formal issuance of the Lost Boys' Call for Peace, Sadiq al-Mahdi had returned to Sudan and published his own apology for the suffering caused during his tenure as prime minister.

Undeniably, what happened on 9/11 was a horrible blow to those of us working for peace between Muslims and Christians. But we would be wrong to give up hope. I thought often in those days of a quotation from Archbishop Oscar Romero of El Salvador, who proclaimed during the darkest days of terror in his country: "Let us not be disheartened, . . . as though human realities made impossible the accomplishment of God's plans."[6]

And I thought of the Lost Boys themselves, who never gave up hope despite their sufferings and setbacks—and who in fact had learned to use them for strength. "We have a unique opportunity, which God has given us," said Abraham. "My hope and prayer is that through long suffering, God has granted us this time to learn, to find creative ideas. Our goal must be to return to the Sudan to help our people."

Though they referred often to the sadness of having lost their families when they were small children, the Lost Boys know a deeper truth. As Abraham shared once during a Bible study,

"Even though we have been separated from our parents, we were never separated from God." Carefully holding the Bible that he had carried all the way from Ethiopia when he was eleven years old, Abraham had voiced the words that found their way into the Lost Boys' Call for Peace: "I've been called a 'lost boy,' but I'm not lost from God."

CHAPTER SIX

Stars in the East

The rubble of the World Trade Center was still warm when Carolyn and I headed for the Middle East in October 2001. We had been stunned along with the rest of the world by the events of 9/11. But, moved by the tragedy to intensify our passion for peace, we were determined not to let fear take control of us. From long experience, we understood that the best way to avoid the paralysis of fear was to take initiative through compassionate action. We still held to the biblical truth that "perfect love casts out fear" (1 John 4:18), and we believed that this was a reality all of us in the United States needed to rediscover with deeper conviction at such a critical moment in our history.

It had been twenty-five years since I had helped Millard and Linda Fuller launch Habitat for Humanity. In that quarter of a century, Habitat had built over 50,000 homes in the United States and 175,000 in more than a hundred other countries. As the idea caught on around the globe, I saw time after time how working together to build affordable homes bridged differences and led to understanding, becoming concrete evidence of love replacing fear.

For weeks in the fall of 2001, Carolyn and I, along with newly hired members of the Habitat staff, explored rural corners of Lebanon and Jordan, visiting potential sites for new Habitat projects. Habitat's International Board of Directors hadn't yet decided whether to attempt housing efforts in these predominantly Muslim countries. Some members felt that the risks were simply too great, and now Al-Qaeda seemed to have ended all chances of our proving otherwise.

But as we met hundreds of people in villages throughout Lebanon and Jordan, we found a reality very different from the images being conveyed endlessly by the media back home. Wherever we went, we were moved by the warm hospitality and sympathy of the people. "We are very sorry for the American people, who have suffered at the hands of violent men," we heard them say over and over. "We know how it is to suffer from such people!" I sent a steady stream of emails back to friends at Habitat headquarters in Americus, Georgia, stating that what we were finding was very different from public perceptions in the U.S. and urging them to take a leap of faith.

Before heading back home, Carolyn and I stopped in Egypt, where Habitat had already been active for more than a decade. We visited almost a hundred families along the Upper Nile River. Some of them were still living in pitifully wretched mud shelters. But others were in brightly colored new Habitat houses. Christian and Muslim families proudly told of how they had helped one another build their new homes, and all of them showed us generous hospitality and treated us with the greatest possible warmth and respect.

Early in November, we said good-bye to our Egyptian friends and left for home. Carolyn and I were tired, but we were encouraged by the reception we had received throughout our visits in the Middle East. As we sank back into our seats for the long flight, I was very much aware that Habitat's board of directors was gathering for a meeting. On the agenda was the controversial proposal to approve the projects in Lebanon and Jordan.

Not long into the first leg of our journey, an emergency announcement came over the airliner's intercom: "If there are any doctors aboard this flight, please report to the flight attendants immediately!" Two men sitting right next to me got up and hurried down the aisle. As we flew through the darkness over the North Atlantic, their seats remained empty, and we wondered what unfolding health crisis kept them occupied.

Then, as we were passing over southern Greenland, the tension was broken by another announcement: "This is your captain speaking. Please welcome a new passenger onto Flight 111. Hany was just born in the back of the plane, and his mother is fine!" The plane's occupants burst into vigorous applause. Carolyn and I took that as a beautiful sign of hope, a sign that God hadn't given up on us yet!

The final leg of our trip was from Chicago to Atlanta. En route between the world's two busiest airports, we were the only passengers in the economy-class section, having declined the invitation to join the other five passengers in the first-class area at the front of the plane. In the wake of 9/11, we were eerily alone in the middle of several hundred vacant seats, the only occupants of a large flying room emptied by fear.

Carolyn and I arrived home to the joyful news that the Habitat for Humanity board had approved the projects in Lebanon and Jordan a few hours before—just about the time little Hany had entered the world in that dark sky 40,000 feet above Greenland. Faith had overcome fear again! Our trip had been a success, and our mission seemed clearer than ever: to work together with other people of faith to counter the demons of fear that threaten us all.

Seven months later, in May 2002, eight of us from Jubilee traveled to Jordan and saw the first Habitat site that resulted from the board's decision. We could hardly have imagined a more perfect setting in which to confront the demons of fear than Al Himmeh, perched on the northern edge of Jordan, with the Israeli-occupied Golan Heights towering above it to the north and the ruins of the ancient city of Gadara to the south. The Sea of Galilee glistened in the sunlight less than four miles away. Carolyn and I had visited Al Himmeh briefly during our 2001 trip, and we had worked on what became the very first Habitat house in Jordan. Now, the eight of us from Jubilee made up the first Habitat work team to come from outside Jordan.

The splendid Habitat staff in Jordan set up the trip for us and worked with us throughout the week. We had the privilege of working on the home of a very poor family with three small children. Um Abdallah, the mother, seemed to be everywhere at once—taking care of her children, jumping in briefly to help mix concrete, serving sweet hot tea every few minutes. All the while she managed to care for her severely disabled five-year-old son, Abdallah. One of the special blessings for the Jubilee people was relating to this little boy, which seemed especially to surprise and please the local people.

Um Abdallah's house was located just 200 yards from a cliff mentioned by the Gospel writers Matthew and Luke. It was over this cliff that the herd of pigs most likely plunged after Jesus sent the legion of demons into them. Yes, this was a perfect place to confront those demons of fear that still plague us twenty centuries later!

The village of Al Himmeh is named for hot springs that pour out of the ground in its center. Visitors have come since ancient times to bathe in its steaming pools. For a little while, however, the Jubilee workers were the biggest show in town.

The Jordanians responded to our coming with extraordinary warmth and hospitality. The children study English in their schools, so each day we heard a chorus of voices shouting, "Welcome to Jordan!" as we walked to work. The people of Al Himmeh have very little money, but they shared what they had with smiles and great generosity.

We were treated to one delicious meal after another throughout our week in their village. People came by the work site with trays of cold drinks for us that must have cost at least a day or two of their income. Others brought produce from their gardens or hot bread, fresh from their outdoor ovens.

The leader of the village, Abu Mohammed, took us on a tour of nearby Pella, the biblical city to which the Christians fled in 70 A.D. when Jerusalem was destroyed by the Romans. Then he hosted us at a banquet and at a special party the final evening. It is hard to imagine how we could have been treated more generously anywhere in the world.

Throughout the week, there was a steady stream of Jordanian college students, professors, social workers, medical people, and others who drove sixty miles from Amman to be with us for a few hours. Near the end of the week there was a flurry of excitement out in the little street next to where we were working. Her Royal Highness Princess Majda Raad had arrived with her entourage of guards and officials. She had come all the way from Amman to thank us for our gesture of friendship from North America to Jordan. Her visit to this home with a disabled child was especially appropriate, because she is an active promoter of care for people with disabilities throughout Jordan.

A little over a year later, in September 2003, I journeyed back to Lebanon, a trip made riskier by the U.S. invasion of Iraq a few months earlier. I was met at the Beirut airport by David Haskell, Habitat for Humanity's Middle East regional director, and Lebanon director Zahi Azar. In my experience, Zahi always had a twinkle in his eye, but I could see that he was up to something special this time.

"I know you expected to keep a very low profile during this visit," he said, "but I have a little suggestion. You can say no, of course." Zahi proposed that we drop off our bags at the hotel in Beirut where we were staying and go immediately into the mountains of southern Lebanon. There we would join a work crew putting the finishing touches on the one hundredth house built or restored there since Habitat began working in partnership with Dialogue and Development, a Lebanese nonprofit organization active in southern Lebanon.

Zahi added, "Then—and you can say no, of course—I suggest

that both of you speak tonight at the dedication service. There may be a few hundred people there, you understand, new Muslim and Christian homeowners. We have not even mentioned that you would be in the country, of course. That might, uh, lead to trouble."

Zahi did not elaborate on the possible "trouble." David and I were fully aware that the work site and the dedication service were in the middle of an area where sectarian militias had fought each other for years, between attacks from Israel just to the south. To put it mildly, it was not a particularly healthy place for U.S. citizens to wander around, especially given the deep resentment felt by most of the local people against the recent policies and pronouncements coming out of Washington.

We expressed our concern for the local Habitat people who might be jeopardized by our presence or by some diplomatic error we might make while speaking at such a large public gathering. Zahi insisted that he and the other Lebanese partners were ready to take that chance. Within an hour, we were driving past the Sabra and Shatila refugee camps, where nearly a thousand Palestinians had been massacred in 1982, and along the Mediterranean coast south of Beirut. We could only trust that Zahi knew what he was doing.

When we reached Sidon, we turned inland and began to wind through the hills overlooking the city. We came to a construction site, where about fifteen people were stacking blocks and shoveling dirt in front of a newly restored house. Thousands of concrete skeletons of houses dot the landscape of Lebanon, testimony to the numerous sectarian battles and Israeli bombing raids since 1982. Habitat's work there usually consists of restoration rather than new construction.

As we left the car and started helping them, several of the workers ran for cameras and began to take pictures of this unexpected sight. John and Therese, the homeowners, hurried inside and began to prepare for a tea break almost before we got started.

After a grand total of about ten minutes of work, they called us all into the house and passed around the little glasses of sweet, hot tea.

Zahi turned to me with that telltale twinkle in his eyes and said, "Don, they would like to hear about the work of Jubilee, especially about the way you took medicine to the Iraqi children." For the next half hour I told about Jubilee's refugee work, emphasizing that we host people of all faiths, without any discrimination. I explained how we had delivered more than twenty truckloads of medicine to the children's hospitals in Iraq in the past few years, and how this had recently expanded into a national program sponsored by thousands of U.S. churches and mosques. In the earlier days, it had been necessary to do this work of mercy without permission from the U.S. government. "But," I insisted, "there should never be a law against saving the lives of children." There were nods and murmurs of agreement all around the room.

We said good-bye to our new friends and drove to a meeting with one of Lebanon's most outstanding men, Bishop Salim Ghazal—"the Nelson Mandela of Lebanon," as David likes to describe him. When Carolyn and I met him on our earlier visit, he had just agreed to serve as chair of the proposed Habitat National Committee, a bold act of faith altogether characteristic of him. We joined him in his Center for Dialogue and Development, a two-story white building on the top of a mountain overlooking Sidon and the Mediterranean Sea.

Bishop Ghazal was acutely aware that if the evening's celebration went well, it would be an important landmark in the work of healing relations between local communities from a variety of religious backgrounds and ethnic groups that had been divided by years of conflict. It would also confirm that he had not blundered in associating himself with Habitat, an organization that, while in reality increasingly international, was still regarded by many people as an American institution.

The evening went well. It went incredibly well! The center's auditorium was filled with that mix of people found only in Lebanon, some dressed in traditional Middle Eastern clothing, some in the latest European fashions. It was a sophisticated audience, Muslim and Christian, all of them undoubtedly hoping that this night would be a significant departure from the strained relations of the past twenty-one years that had marked their lives since their country had fractured along sectarian lines.

As I waited for my turn to speak, I looked out over the crowd and felt a wave of gratitude to be trusted and welcomed by these people who had suffered so much from war, and who had chosen to put that behind them and help one another build new homes. I spoke about how Habitat for Humanity had grown out of a situation in the American South where people had also suffered from deep divisions, how it was intended from the first to be about reconciliation and love between people and not simply about building houses.

As Zahi translated from English to Arabic, I could see that he was conveying the spirit of what I said as well as the words. The people responded enthusiastically. They responded even more enthusiastically to David's message, delivered directly in Arabic, and to the closing comments from Salim Ghazal.

The evening was off to a good start, but it soon got even better. Lebanon is famous for its fine food, and that night there was a potluck banquet unlike anything I had ever seen! I filled my plate with exotic samples. I didn't know what to call them, but the pleasant and pungent aromas made the names irrelevant.

I was about to sit down to eat when music boomed out so loudly that I'm sure people could hear it at least a mile from the mountaintop in all directions. Huge outdoor speakers had been raised on tall stands in front of the center. A powerful sound system began to play passionate music that immediately reminded me of the medieval Latin cantata *Carmina Burana,* with a Middle Eastern accent.

"Lebanese folk music," someone shouted in my ear. "We

dance." Seconds later I was pulled to a clear area out near the road and inserted into the traditional line dance. The other dancers looked very graceful as they swayed and did their intricate side steps in a long line. I stomped along with them as well as I could, still in my work boots, but it was obvious that the big crowd appreciated my clumsy efforts.

"Now *that's* real dialogue," Bishop Ghazal said as he watched approvingly. David was much better at it than I, and we spent much of the next two hours alternating between our food and our work of dance-floor diplomacy. This had become anything but a "low profile" visit!

Policemen stood at the edge of the big crowd to ensure that there would be no incidents. I went over to them and thanked them for their attention. "No problem at all," one said pleasantly. "But where is the other American? We've lost sight of him." I helped them to find David in the crowd, and they relaxed again.

Several people went to the microphone and praised Bishop Ghazal for working courageously for peace year after year. One woman shouted with emotion over the P.A. system, "Tonight good-will and our ancient tradition of mutual help between neighbors have returned to Lebanon for the first time in a generation!" It was obvious that all the happy celebrants agreed with her. I felt such joy to have played a small part in this beautiful event, which I would-n't have missed even if the danger had been ten times greater.

Just before leaving Lebanon the next day, David and I visited Bishop Salim Ghazal one more time. He was ecstatic. "The tele-phone has been ringing all morning," he told us, "with people expressing their appreciation for last night and wanting to know what they can do next to help. Even one of our most outspoken skeptics, a professor from Sidon, called us to say that he heard you speak at the building site and then came to the celebration last night. He told us that he will be a vigorous supporter from now on. He even promised to put that in writing so that we can use it for promotional purposes."

David and I had to rush to the airport for our flight to Egypt. But we knew that we would never forget the mountaintop miracle of community building and reconciliation we had witnessed in south Lebanon.

In Cairo, Carolyn was waiting with ten other people we had recruited as a special work delegation. They were mostly long-time friends. Half the group had lived during the early 1970s at Koinonia Partners. Linda Fuller was among them, as thrilled as I was to see the group that had grown out of a brief chat we'd had six months earlier. The rest were mostly Habitat leaders from around the United States. Our mission was to work together as a team in Egypt and Jordan and then go back and help promote the work of Habitat for Humanity in the Middle East and organize other work teams to these countries.

On our first day in Egypt, Yousry Makar joined us at the Baron Hotel for breakfast. I introduced him to our group, and he welcomed us to his country. He suggested that we all gather our luggage and meet the chartered bus at the front of the hotel. From there we went to the Habitat headquarters, met his staff, and were briefed about Habitat in Egypt. After lunch, we piled back into the bus and set out on the four-hour trip to the large Upper Nile city of El Minya.

We crossed the Nile and passed the famous Giza pyramids, heading toward the desert highway that runs parallel to the river about ten miles to the west. As we were leaving the edge of Cairo, we had to stop at a police station. There we became a conspicuous caravan, with military escorts fore and aft. One double-cab pickup truck raced ahead of us, with siren screaming and lights flashing. It carried eight soldiers, all armed with AK-47s. A second truck followed us, bringing six or eight more heavily armed guards.

We understood why all this attention was required by the Egyptian government. In November 1997, members of an extremist group named al-Gama'a al-Islamiya opened fire on a group of foreign tourists, killing fifty-eight of them, at Luxor, an Upper Nile city not far from where we were heading. This terrible act also took a broad toll on the Egyptian people. Hundreds of thousands of poor families whose livelihoods depended on tourism, until then a multibillion-dollar industry in Egypt, became unemployed overnight. The Upper Nile region was particularly hard hit.

Government officials were eager to resurrect the tourist industry, and they were determined to prevent any repetition of violence against international visitors. They welcomed a group like ours that was blazing the trail once more to sites in Upper Egypt. We had very mixed feelings, to say the least, about being guarded by soldiers at all times. Our purpose was to reach out in friendship to the people around us, and they unfailingly responded with warm smiles and greetings. We were wondering how we could have much natural interaction with them with a platoon of soldiers around us holding their submachine guns at the ready.

Perhaps not surprisingly, in the wake of the shocking incident in Luxor, Habitat for Humanity work delegations to Egypt had also come to a screeching halt along with tourism. I had increased my efforts to organize work groups, speaking frequently throughout the United States and Canada. The possibility of at least six delegations had emerged from that endeavor, but then the U.S. war against Iraq stopped all but one of them. A group of courageous Canadians from Manitoba had come in January 2003. Our delegation was the first to come from the U.S. in the six years since the Luxor attack.

All of us were aware that our visit had special significance because of the anti-American sentiment that had spread through Egypt and the rest of the Middle East since the U.S. invasion of Iraq. We were scheduled to spend only a day and a half on construction sites, but everyone understood that our visit was more important as a symbol of healing in relationships than for any physical work we would do. The normally warm relations between Egyptians and Americans had been strained by the war, by statements from Washington, and by images in our media that painted the entire Arab world with the broad brush of terrorism.

In El Minya, a major city on the Upper Nile, we attended a gathering of leaders from the local villages with Habitat projects. One after another they proudly gave their reports. "Our goal was to build and repair one hundred and fifty houses in two years," said the Muslim leader from Susha. "Instead, we have reached three hundred houses!" He smiled with pride as everyone applauded enthusiastically. "And our repayment rate is one hundred percent!" More applause came for this amazing achievement of every house loan being repaid in a region where the economy is in such a shambles. And so it went, with speaker after speaker telling how Habitat had helped them rebuild their communities and restore hope in places of angry frustration.

For me, the high point of our trip to Egypt came at the end of this meeting. Farid, the leader who had given the report for the town of El Tayeba, indicated that he would like Yousry to translate for him as he told me something. Looking me in the eye and speaking with great dignity, he said, "I would like to tell you that the visit of your group to our communities is not less significant than the visits of [the apostle] Paul to encourage the scattered Christians of his day."

I was so moved by Farid's statement that I fumbled for something to say in response to his eloquence. But I could only get out, "Thank you for your hospitality. The honor is ours."

After a night in the Cleopatra Hotel in El Minya, we went the remaining few miles to the village of Bany Mohammed Sha'rawy. Like scores of other villages in the region, this one was a collection of tightly crowded houses on the bank of the Nile, surrounded by rich farmland right up to the walls of the outermost homes. A few thousand residents lived in an area of no more than fifty or sixty acres. The village had been chosen as a site for a major Habitat project not only because of its many deteriorating houses, but also because of the cooperative spirit of the Muslim and Christian leaders of the community.

Our conspicuous caravan raced through the open country and into the walled courtyard where the village leaders waited to greet us. The soldiers scattered around the courtyard, rifles in hand. After half an hour of formal greetings and hot tea all around, we moved outside to go to our work sites.

Yousry explained to us that we would be divided among four work crews, each assigned to a different Habitat house under construction. I was to help pour a concrete roof on a two-story house near the northern edge of the village. On the same crew would be Ron Thomas, the energetic director of the Habitat affiliate in Port Charlotte, Florida, and Steve Clemens, an old friend with whom I had worked on many a project over the years.

The forms and steel reinforcements were all in place for the roof. After a bit of organizing with our half-dozen local coworkers—always an adventure in communication across the language barrier—we got to work. Steve remained on the roof with two of the other men to spread and smooth the concrete. Others worked on the ground in the courtyard of the house next door, mixing the concrete and shoveling it into buckets. Ron and I volunteered to be the "conveyor belt," carrying the buckets up to the roof on our shoulders.

We soon fell into a smooth routine. Swinging the full buckets to our shoulders, Ron and I stepped through the gate of the courtyard and into the narrow street, took a few steps to our right, entered the front door of the Habitat house, went up a flight of stairs, climbed a ladder to the roof, dumped the concrete, and then headed down for the next load. We kept a steady rhythm, shuttling one load after another, one of us going up while the other was coming back down.

It was hot work—and strenuous. Both Ron and I were in good physical condition, but it was a real workout to keep up with the mixers on the ground and the troweling team on the roof. All thoughts of regional politics, our armed guards, and such things were crowded out by the satisfying physical work with our new Egyptian friends. There was lots of good-natured banter, and a constant audience of curious children watching the Americans sweat.

As we worked, I was very conscious that just a few miles farther up the Nile was the place where my life had been profoundly affected more than four decades earlier by my encounter with Lillian Trasher. In 1960, I had been a 21-year-old privileged son of a wealthy businessman. I had become utterly turned off by the kind of religious background in which I had been raised, with its constant drumbeat of hellfire and brimstone, its emotional appeals to fear, its racist and militaristic assumptions, and an almost total disregard for the Gospel's social dimensions. I was running from that as hard as I could.

I spent five months biking across Europe and walking, hitchhiking, and traveling as cheaply as possible around the Middle East. My wild adventures (some of them pretty stupid and dangerous) were part of the escape attempt. On my way up the Nile on a third-class train, I remembered that for a couple of years I had sent five dollars every month to the Lillian Trasher Orphanage in Assiout, Egypt. I got off the train in Assiout, walked across a bridge to the orphanage on the east bank of the Nile, knocked on its big gate, and announced that I'd like to see Lillian Trasher.

I waited while someone went to call "Mama Lillian." Not only did she come to see this ragged and brash young visitor, she welcomed me as though I were her own son. Undoubtedly she had done the same for thousands of other young people and children over the years. I didn't know at that moment that I was about to have one of the most important experiences of my life.

I'm sure it was obvious by the time I reached Assiout that I had been on the road a long time. With a broad smile, Lillian proclaimed, "You are dirty! Come with me, and I will show you where you can bathe and put on some clean clothes." After nearly half a century I still remember very clearly that first meeting with her. I was immediately impressed by two things: she was full of love and she was so joyful! I had never before met anyone who radiated such love and such joy.

During the next forty-eight hours Lillian Trasher gave me a whole new picture of what it means to be a Christian. I was a self-ish young man from a rich family in a rich nation, and I knew hardly anything at all about the hunger and suffering of other people. But in those two days with Mama Lillian, my life started to change. I began to understand that Jesus taught his followers to serve other people. I started to realize that true joy and fulfillment do not come from power or money, but from recognizing that God loves all of us and invites us to live in peace as brothers and sisters.

For two wonderful days, I followed Mama Lillian around the orphanage compound, eating all my meals with her and talking with her by the hour. A big crowd followed her everywhere. People just liked to be near her. She was so full of life that I never suspected that she had already suffered a couple of heart attacks, and I couldn't have imagined that she would be dead within a year, at the age of 76.

Now, in the courtyard in Bany Mohammed Sha'rawy over forty years later, I was remembering Lillian Trasher and pondering what an exciting mystery God's work is in our lives. Little did I suspect that I was about to have another experience so astonishing that I am still struggling to comprehend its full significance.

The mixing crew filled my bucket again, and I swung it up onto my shoulder. I stepped through the gate into the narrow street and turned to my right. Most of that morning the street had been empty, but now I found myself facing four men striding toward me, shoulder to shoulder. They were in their late 20s or early 30s, and all were dressed in galabeyas, the long robes typical of rural

Egypt, and head coverings. When they were no more than eight or ten feet from me, the one second from the left raised a rifle from beside his robe, crouched, and aimed it right in my face.

At that point a series of miracles took place that disarmed the situation as surely as God closed the mouths of those lions around Daniel in Babylon. First, contrary to what would have been a normal response, I was absolutely clear and totally calm. At no time during or after the incident did I feel even a trace of fear. As I stared down the muzzle of the rifle, I thought, with total detachment, "This may be the end." Then, in a ludicrous afterthought, "That's a little larger than a twenty-two-caliber rifle, but not quite as large as my old two-seventy Savage hunting rifle."

Next—and all this happened in the space of a second or two—I called up some of the very few words I knew in Arabic. I said with a big smile as I waved my free hand, "Salaam alikim. La, la, la!" or "Peace to you. No, no, no!" And I kept right on walking with my bucket of concrete without missing a step. The men stepped back in surprise, and then a moment later awkward smiles spread over their startled faces. The one with the rifle lowered it as I walked past him and went on with my business.

I have no idea where they went after that, because, as strange as it seems to me now, I instantly forgot the incident. I carried my load of concrete up to the roof and dumped it. It never crossed my mind to alert Steve and the others that there were men down in the street with a rifle. It never occurred to me to try to get the attention of the soldiers who were all over the village. In fact, I didn't even think to look around for the men as I went back through the street a minute later to get my next bucket of concrete.

A little while later, Ron and I took a rest break beside the mixing area in the courtyard. As we leaned back against a wall in the shade, wiping the sweat from our faces, Ron turned and asked me, "Don, did anything strange happen to you a little while ago?"

I had to think for a minute. Then I said, "Yeah, four guys pointed what looked like a rifle right in my face!"

"Same thing happened to me," Ron answered calmly.

"Really! And what did you do?"

"Oh, I just smiled at them," he said. "I said something like, 'Hello. No, no, no.' Then I just kept on working. I forgot all about it until just a minute ago."

Incredibly, Ron and I then forgot the whole matter again. When our team assembled for lunch, we never thought to say anything to the others. Carolyn says that if I mentioned it to her, she must have forgotten it just as promptly as Ron and I did.

It was not until I was back home in my office weeks later that these events began to flood back into my mind. At first, I was suspicious that I might have imagined them. I called Ron Thomas to see if he also remembered them. He did. But, as in my case, he had found them mysteriously elusive memories, especially while we were still in the Middle East. Like me, he had a tendency to shrug the whole matter off as something inconsequential that had taken place in a matter of two or three minutes in a back street of a remote Egyptian village.

Not Yousry Makar! When I sent an email to Yousry—"Just thought you might be interested"—he called me immediately from Egypt. "Don," he said emphatically, "this is very important! Even if those men were somehow intending that as a joke, it is extremely serious. We must find out immediately what was going on. I am going to talk to some of the men that I know very well in Bany Mohammed Sha'rawy. I will tell you what I find out."

Yousry's friends were as shocked by the story as he had been. They insisted that they knew everyone in the village and that no one there would have done what we described, not even as a bad joke. First, it would have amounted to suicide if any of the government soldiers had seen it happen. Second, it would have jeopardized the entire Habitat program in the region, something for which they all felt great gratitude and pride. And most fundamentally, such a gesture—if it had been intended somehow as a joke—would have been an unthinkable insult to guests for whom the whole village was extending their warm hospitality.

"No," they insisted, "these men could not have been from Bany Mohammed Sha'rawy!" The mystery still remains as to who those men were and what they intended toward us.

In sharp contrast, the people of the village went all out to make clear to us that we were very welcome among them. Children gave us flowers, local leaders made speeches, and we were served round after round of sweet tea so hot we could barely hold the little glasses. Our hosts were as aware as we were that our visit represented a small but important step back toward warm friendship between the people of Egypt and the United States.

Several mentioned how hard times had been for them when the tourist business plunged to almost nothing. Our visit was big news. A television cameraman spent hours filming the unusual sight of Americans mixing concrete, hammering, plastering, and sweating alongside local Egyptians. "Even when we had lots of American tourists before the trouble," one man told me, "they just wore big hats and took pictures. I have never seen Americans work like this."

At the end of our stay in Egypt, we enjoyed a beautiful reception at the headquarters of the Coptic Evangelical Organization for Social Services in Cairo, as the guests of Nabil Abadir. Nabil is the executive director of CEOSS and was a fellow member of Habitat's International Board of Directors. He is a genuine peacemaker who serves as a beautiful example of Christian leadership under very difficult circumstances. Soon afterward, we reluctantly said good-bye to Yousry and the rest of his excellent Habitat staff and headed to the Cairo airport for the brief flight to Amman, Jordan.

It was already well after dark as we departed. In an hour we crossed the wilderness in which Moses and his followers had wandered for forty years. We landed at the main international airport for Jordan, just fifteen miles from Mount Nebo, from which Moses had looked over the broad Jordan Valley and glimpsed the Promised Land that he would not reach. At the foot of this mountain, he had spoken the words of God to God's people: "I have set before you life and death, blessings and curses. Choose life so that you and your descendants may live" (Deuteronomy 30:19, NRSV).

The Jordan Director of Habitat for Humanity, Philip Griffith, met us at the airport. Philip is a North American who has spent most of his life in the Middle East. He radiates enthusiasm and determination to put his faith into effective action. We climbed aboard a bus and arrived late at night at the hotel in Amman.

The next morning, after an orientation session at the hotel with Philip and his staff, we piled into the bus again and rode north to the border with Israel and Syria. A few minutes from our destination, we came to one of the most dramatic panoramas in the Middle East. On a rocky hilltop, we stood among the Greek and Roman ruins of Gadara, one of the Decapolis cities in the Bible. We looked out over terrain that has likely seen more famous spiritual and historical events in the past several millennia than any other spot on earth of equal size.

The Sea of Galilee lay five miles to the northwest. Along its southern shore were several Israeli *kibbutzim,* including one where I had worked for ten days in 1960 and again in 1962. Just south of them in the Jordan Valley lay the West Bank, with the still-bleeding Palestinian town of Jenin, where many people had been killed by Israeli forces the previous year, just before the visit by our Jubilee delegation.

Southern Lebanon lay to the northwest in the haze beyond the lake, and I smiled as I remembered our celebration in those very hills just one week earlier. The Golan Heights rose high above the Yarmuk Valley, directly across from where we stood. Off to the right we could see out across the deserts of Syria and the western end of the Fertile Crescent.

Many of the best-known events of Jesus' life had taken place among the fields and ridges that lay before us. Down below us, where the slopes of Gadara meet the Golan Heights, lay our des-

113

tination, the village of Al Himmeh. I recalled working there on Jordan's first Habitat house with Carolyn exactly two years earlier, and then on Um Abdallah's house with the Jubilee team a few months later.

My memories of our previous visits made me feel that I would be very much at home in Al Himmeh. That was confirmed when we arrived at the little Habitat staff house and I saw the village leader, Abu Mohammed, coming to greet us. "My friend," he called out, smiling broadly.

These two words make up a sizeable part of Abu Mohammed's total English vocabulary, but they are a good beginning. My Arabic is about as extensive as his English, but we are, in fact, good friends. Abu Mohammed approached me with his arms spread and hugged me with a dramatic flourish. As I introduced each of the members of our group, he welcomed them warmly.

As in Egypt, our group's visit was more important as a gesture of goodwill than for any actual construction work we might accomplish. Our hosts knew this as well as we did. And they had far more at stake. The little valley where they lived was a political caldron between Jordan and Syria on one side and the Israeli troops on the Golan Heights above them on the other. Living there was a bit like trying to raise one's family on the median of a busy four-lane highway—or under a dangerous and busy flight path, as we would soon discover.

The 2,000 permanent residents of Al Himmeh are all Muslims, but they give themselves wholeheartedly in hospitality to Christians as well as to other Muslims. As on our earlier visits, we were greeted with broad smiles and invitations to tea wherever we went. The people of Al Himmeh are generous, sincere hosts. The children are absolutely beautiful, and they seemed never to miss a chance to shout "Hello! Welcome!"

The painful irony is that I had received the same kind of hospitality from Israeli *kibbutzniks* less than ten miles from Al Himmeh. There, beautiful, smiling Jewish children had eagerly practiced their English words on me just as these beautiful Arab children were now. I had quickly grown to love the Israelis, and I continue to value friendships with them that have survived nearly half a century and countless political arguments. As I pondered the irony, I whispered a prayer into the wind: "Dear God, these people you have created on both sides of the border must somehow discover that they have more to love in each other than to fear. We all need desperately to learn that about one another."

But fear and international conflict were to dominate the news throughout our week in Al Himmeh. At just about the time that we were looking out from the hilltop ruins of Gadara across the lovely Jordan River valley, a young Palestinian woman from Jenin was walking into a crowded restaurant in Haifa, Israel, just out of our sight to the west, with powerful explosives strapped to her body. She detonated the bomb and killed eighteen other people as she ended her own brief life.

The next afternoon we were hard at work on the house we had come to build. I was up on a scaffold laying blocks when someone signaled to me that I had a telephone call. I took the cell phone and walked out among the olive trees to get away from the noise at the building site.

"Don, I have bad news. Israel has just bombed a site on the north edge of Damascus, not far from where you are working." It was Philip calling from the Habitat office in Amman. "This is the first Israeli attack on Syrian territory in thirty years," he continued. "The United Nations Security Council is in emergency session about it right now." Philip and I discussed the situation for a few minutes. He assured me that he would keep on top of the news and call immediately if it appeared that we should leave the area.

I kept the news to myself for an hour, until we finished the day's work and could talk privately among the members of our group and the Habitat staff. I described the situation to them, stressing that anyone who felt they had to leave the area was free to do so and that we would arrange transportation at once. After a brief discussion, every person in the group said that he or she wanted to continue with what we had come to do, unless it became obvious that we had to leave. At that moment I felt prouder than ever of this group of serious peacemakers and very privileged to call them friends.

That evening Linda Fuller called Millard at the Habitat for Humanity headquarters back in Americus, Georgia. He affirmed our decision and assured us that he and the others at the office would be praying for our safety and for all the people in the conflict zone.

Our delegation was staying in the little staff house on the edge of Al Himmeh. All of us slept on mattresses scattered on the floor and under mosquito nets. The weather was even hotter than normal on the edge of the desert, and we had trouble sleeping. After the first night we began to move our beds one by one up a long ladder and onto the flat roof of the building. It was far more comfortable, and the stars overhead were stunningly beautiful.

On the third night, I was on the roof when I was suddenly awakened by a brilliant flash of light. I checked my watch. It was 1:30 A.M. I lay under my net for a few seconds trying to grasp what had happened, when suddenly the whole hillside around me was as bright as day. Then darkness again, just as suddenly. I ripped my net back and sat up.

A powerful beam of light swept the area again. I looked back over my shoulder and saw that the searchlight was coming from an Israeli bunker up on the Golan Heights. Back and forth it swept, all over the sleeping village of Al Himmeh, sometimes lighting an area the size of a city block, sometimes focusing down in a narrow beam so brilliant that it hurt the eyes of anyone caught looking up in its glare. As it swept over me I felt violated as surely as if someone were hurling stones down from the mountain.

"It happens all the time," shrugged one of the Jordanians the next day. And sometimes, he said, Jordanian soldiers "return the favor," shining lights on Israeli fortifications and vehicles. The next night I looked up just in time to see a bright flare light the sky for a few seconds. It was life as usual along the border, with its constant reminders that each side is always watching for an excuse to shoot or bomb anyone who appears to be a threat.

We continued our work with the Jordanian family we had come to serve. They were extremely poor: a disabled father, an incredibly hard-working mother, a twelve-year-old daughter, and an eleven-year-old son. Their ramshackle old house had been in such bad condition that a large part of the roof had fallen in on them not long before we had arrived. They were thrilled to be getting a new home, and they showed it by their smiles and by working very hard with us.

For a week we mixed concrete, tied steel reinforcement bars into place, laid blocks, and carried a thousand loads of stone and mortar in floppy little containers made from old tires. From time to time we retreated to the shade to drink cups of tea with our hosts. Then we went back to work. The work progressed steadily despite the international tension around us.

In the middle of the week, as we were working on the roof, preparing to cover it with concrete, we were suddenly shaken by sonic booms. Two jets flew directly over us, on a northeastward course from Israel into Syrian airspace. There was a pause in the work, then a word or two between the workers. And then we continued what we were doing. We were getting to be old hands at this.

We finished the house right on schedule. As we smoothed the last of the concrete on the roof with trowels, cars began to arrive with official visitors from Al Himmeh and surrounding towns. We were pleased but not too surprised to see Abu Mohammed arrive, enthusiastically touring the new house and congratulating the family.

Then the mayors of other towns in the region arrived, some having come quite a distance to participate in the dedication of this little house. Finally, there was a special flurry of excitement as one large black car pulled into the crowded parking area. The word went around, "The governor of northern Jordan has come to celebrate with us!"

One by one, local leaders expressed their appreciation for our work under the hot sun on a house for a poor Jordanian family. We made appropriately modest responses as they insisted that they had never seen people come from so far away and work so hard for their community. The governor made the closing speech.

"This week," he said, "we have all been aware of the tensions between neighboring countries, of the possibility of great trouble. But here on this hillside in Al Himmeh, we have seen an encouraging sight. We have seen people who do not even speak the same language working side by side and becoming friends. Thousands of people all over northern Jordan knew what was happening on this hillside in Al Himmeh. This gives all of us hope that we can someday have real peace in the Middle East."

We returned home two days later, tired but more convinced than ever before that there can be peace instead of war in this world—if we make the choice for "life and blessing" that Moses put before the people. God still puts that choice before us all. And, as Moses insisted, *it is not too hard for us.* It's actually the most exciting way to live there is!

CHAPTER SEVEN

Groundbreaking Faith

"I am about to do a new thing; now it springs forth, do you not perceive it?"

—Isaiah 43:19, NRSV

Istood on a picturesque hillside under a brilliantly gleaming sun, imagining a checkerboard of passive-solar-design duplexes coming to life there. I had carried a similar dream to many places before, but I felt something extraordinary in the hope for it in this space. I was standing in the middle of a tree nursery at Osan-ri, just two miles east of North Korea's Pyongyang Airport.

As I envisioned the possibilities there, I recalled the many conversations with people who had responded to my announcement of this trip with, "You're going where?" For decades, the Democratic People's Republic of Korea (North Korea) has been on our nation's official enemies list, and former President George W. Bush pronounced it part of the "axis of evil," keeping company with Iraq and Iran as the nations he and a host of supporters have labeled the most dangerous on earth. But for every person who was aghast upon hearing the news of my destination, several responded with enthusiasm about this groundbreaking venture.

Under that bright sun, I was mindful of the very long journey,

and the multiple challenges and complications that had to be con-
quered, to get to that hillside. In a sense, it began more than four
decades ago. Ever since Carolyn and I went to the southern half
of Korea as young newlyweds in the summer of 1967, we have
felt a special love for the people of this culturally rich but embat-
tled peninsula.

Our two years there were among the most challenging we have
ever experienced, as I struggled to supervise more than a hundred
Peace Corps volunteers working in Seoul and in remote towns
and villages from coast to coast along the demilitarized zone.
Tensions were constantly high as South Korean president Park
Chung Hee became increasingly repressive, and as raiding parties
from the north sometimes crossed the DMZ and attacked villages
where I had stationed volunteers in schools and health clinics.

In one especially dramatic week, while we were holding a Peace
Corps conference for our volunteers in a retreat center north of
Seoul, an assassination team of thirty-one North Korean commandos was sneaking through the woods past us toward the South
Korean president's "Blue House." They advanced to within half a
mile of the presidential residence before they were discovered, and
there a frantic battle erupted between them and members of the
South Korean security forces. We pulled the curtains across the
windows, turned off the lights, and crouched in the darkness as the
commandos desperately fought their way back past us, pursued by
the security forces. We collectively held our breath as we watched
flares arcing through the night sky and heard bursts of gunfire all
around us. When it was over, sixty-eight South Koreans and all but
two of the North Koreans were dead.

Two days later, on January 23, 1968, the U.S. spy ship *Pueblo*
was captured off North Korea's east coast. Its crew members
were taken to prisoner-of-war camps near Pyongyang. They
endured torture, starvation, and mock executions for eleven
months before being released.

In the late 1960s, South Korea was extremely impoverished.

The "economic miracle" to come had not yet begun, although our Peace Corps volunteers were helping to lay the groundwork for it. Poor as they were, the Koreans with whom we worked were extraordinarily courageous and determined to make the best of every opportunity.

Despite the war that had divided their country only a few years earlier, and the continual threat of military confrontation, I discovered that the feelings of the Koreans in the south toward those in the north were more complicated and nuanced than I had encountered in other war zones. Military conflicts generally break out between peoples separated by language, culture, politics, and history. By contrast, in South Korea I constantly met people who had relatives north of the DMZ with whom they longed to be reunited. North Korea and South Korea were not so much two different nations as they were two halves of one nation that history had ripped across the middle—and the wound was still fresh and painful.

These memories and observations came back clearly in the early 1990s as I became aware of escalating tensions in the region once again. After the collapse of the Soviet Union, the communist North Koreans were feeling heightened vulnerability. Their government leaders asked the United States to sign a nonaggression pact, but our leaders refused even to discuss it with them. The sense of vulnerability was exacerbated by a growing shortage of food and oil.

It was well known by then that the North Koreans had a small nuclear reactor and were beginning to produce weapons-grade nuclear materials. These included a small but dangerous amount of plutonium. Understandably, this development was making their neighbors nervous, especially South Korea, Japan, and China.

In June 1994, Jimmy Carter—who had been a nuclear engineer before he launched his political career—became concerned enough about the situation that he finally responded affirmatively to the repeated invitations of North Korea's "Great Leader," Kim Il Sung, to come for a face-to-face conversation. Based on his personal discussions with Chinese experts and the U.S. general then commanding American and South Korean military forces, Carter believed that the danger of a major war was very great. In March 2003, in an interview on an edition of public television's *Frontline* titled "Kim's Nuclear Gamble," he reflected back on the potential threat at that time: "It might very well have been a second Korean War, within which a million people or so could have been killed."

Kim Il Sung was clearly impressed by the willingness of Jimmy and Rosalynn Carter to travel to Pyongyang. Their talks resulted in several important agreements. Kim seems to have been genuinely ready to back away from the brinksmanship he was practicing, including allowing international inspectors to supervise the dismantling of the plutonium-processing operation at Yongbyon. But three weeks after these very productive talks, the "Great Leader" died suddenly of a heart attack.

We'll never know what would have happened if Kim Il Sung had lived a few more years, and if Washington had fully followed through on its end of the agreements he worked out with Jimmy Carter. Clinton administration Secretary of State Madeleine Albright, believing like Carter in the importance of bilateral talks, visited Pyongyang in October 2000 and negotiated with Kim Jong Il, the son and successor of Kim Il Sung. But critics labeled such efforts "appeasement," and when George W. Bush took over the presidency, his administration put an immediate halt to all such talks.

In subsequent conversations with Jimmy Carter, I sensed his deep frustration when he described the stubborn refusal of so many in our government to trust at least as much in respectful dialogue with our adversaries as in threats and military force. We talked about the paramount importance of "saving face" among Koreans, given their strong Confucian culture. Not understanding that, our leaders seemed determined to use threats and insults to advance their policies, apparently mystified as to why such tactics had exactly the opposite effect from what they intended.

Even while I was deeply engaged in work for peace in other parts of the world, I couldn't completely put Korea out of my mind. I was particularly concerned about North Korea's growing isolation and the suffering of its people from repression, poverty, and hunger. When I learned in September 2000 that the annual Jimmy Carter Work Project with Habitat for Humanity was going to be in South Korea the following summer, I got a wild idea. What if I were to recruit a group of my old Peace Corps friends with whom I had served in South Korea and simultaneously build a few Habitat houses in North Korea?

I shared the idea with a few of them and got an enthusiastic response. Predictably, both Jimmy Carter and Millard Fuller liked it as well. We eventually managed to get our proposal to officials in Pyongyang, and they also responded positively. Over many months of email correspondence between Peace Corps veterans and Habitat folks, our excitement grew.

Then the word came from the North Koreans that they wanted us to construct an apartment building in their capital city for high-level government officials.

"Oh, no!" I responded when I heard that. "That's not what Habitat does."

Back came the answer, "Then we are not interested."

I felt we had hit a brick wall with the idea, so despite all the effort, I abandoned it. I had plenty of other projects demanding my attention. That summer of 2001 the "lost boys" of Sudan required almost all of our time and energy at Jubilee Partners.

In mid-September I was in Indianapolis for a celebration of Habitat for Humanity's twenty-fifth birthday. Just days after the 9/11 attacks, Jimmy Carter and Millard Fuller delivered eloquent pleas for people to respond with restraint and compassionate action rather than bitter violence. On September 14, Millard came up to me in the hall of the Indianapolis Convention Center and said, "Guess what, Don? The North Koreans have just sent word to me that now they understand what Habitat does." The month before, the volunteers with the Jimmy Carter Work Project had built many houses in several South Korean villages, making a point of locating a dozen of them right next to the DMZ. "They say," continued Millard, "that they would like for you to come ahead and work with them!"

I just shook my head and answered, "No way. Carolyn and I have decided that it is more urgent now for us to go to the Middle East and see if we can help start those Habitat programs in Lebanon and Jordan. North Korea will have to wait."

A month later, Carolyn and I were in the Middle East. A year later, I was elected back onto Habitat for Humanity's International Board of Directors. I had served in that capacity for the first seven years of Habitat's existence, and it felt very good to be back in that role again—until I found myself in the middle of a crescendo of clashes, charges, and countercharges between Millard, Habitat staff members, and the Board. The conflict eventually led to the Board firing Millard and Linda—I believe unjustly, based on the evidence—and to my resigning.

Almost immediately I set out on another trip to the Middle East to help promote the Habitat work there. Within four months, in April 2005, Millard and Linda founded the Fuller Center for Housing, continuing their commitment to provide affordable shelter around the world. I decided to try to help get roofs over people's heads through both Habitat and the Fuller Center.

In October 2006, the North Koreans got my attention again— and that of the rest of the world as well. They conducted a nuclear test. By nuclear standards, it was a tiny explosion, but its implications were huge.

Jubilee Partners member Coffee Worth, who has spent more than twenty of her ninety years on this earth serving as a missionary with her husband George in South Korea, called my attention to a program at the University of Georgia in Athens. Dr. Han S. Park, a leading expert on North Korea, was scheduled to speak just fifteen miles from Jubilee. I decided I needed to hear what he had to say.

Dr. Park is director of the Center for the Study of Global Issues (GLOBIS), headquartered at the University of Georgia campus but with satellite projects in Japan, Italy, and South Africa. He is a world-renowned peacemaker and a captivating speaker with an engaging sense of humor. He pulled no punches when he described what we are up against in today's world: "Today's powerful weapons make conflict resolution essential—or we could see the annihilation of the entire human race."

I was fascinated and deeply moved by Han Park's insights into the philosophy and motivations of the North Koreans. Instead of simply brushing them aside as bloodthirsty or crazy as so many have done, he led us through the convoluted history of the people, their terrible suffering at the hands of one foreign power after another, and their isolation after the collapse of the Soviet Union and the economic transformation in China—all of which has caused them to adopt their fervent allegiance to *Juche,* or self-reliance. "All North Korean policies are designed to help them survive in what they perceive as a dangerous and hostile world where everyone seems out to get them if they lower their guard," Dr. Park said. "Over and over the United States, especially, has said and done the very thing that pushes them deeper into this kind of thinking. What we really should be doing is helping to establish an alternative system of security, one based on a peace-making approach instead of military threat."[1]

By the time Dr. Park had finished his presentation, I knew I wanted to get better acquainted with him. I called him at his office, and he agreed immediately to meet me for lunch a couple of days later. We learned, among other things, that we were born within days of each other, he in northeastern China and I in Waco, Texas. By the time we left the restaurant after our two-hour conversation—with Han literally running down the street to teach his next class—we had agreed to try again to launch a housing project in North Korea. This time I felt sure we would have a far better chance of success than we had with my fumbling attempt five years earlier.

I first proposed the project to the leadership of Habitat for Humanity. They expressed doubts that they could get permission from the U.S. government to undertake such an effort but asked for time to investigate it. Several weeks passed with no further word. Then one day I was talking with Millard on the phone about a completely different matter, when, on an impulse, I said, "Hey, Millard, here's a wild proposal. How would you like to make another attempt to launch a housing project in North Korea, this time sponsored by the Fuller Center?"

It took Millard about half a second to think it over. "You bet! That's a great idea, Don. Go for it, and I'll back you up any way I can!"

Further encouragement came again from Jimmy Carter. In April 2008, I responded to his invitation to join him as an international observer of the first election ever to take place in Nepal, a nation that had been ruled for centuries by a monarchy. I saw it as another opportunity to reach out to the "enemy"—in this case Maoists, who were being blamed for all the violence around the country in the days leading up to the election. Carter rightly pointed out in a news conference that the king's forces had killed more people trying to prevent the election than the Maoists had killed trying to bring it about.

The day before the election, after the most intensive briefing I've ever experienced—learning about Nepali culture, political background, election procedures, observer duties, logistics, security issues, and use of a satellite phone—Carter's son Chip and I set out in a Land Rover with a driver and an interpreter. We were headed to meet with local people in a rural district east of Katmandu, and with the young Maoists they feared would attack polling places, steal ballot boxes, and disrupt the voting. The Maoists assured us that their goal of including women and "untouchables" in the political process had already been achieved, and that they would not be involved in disruptive violence the next day.

On Election Day, our top priority was to station ourselves at one of the remote sites where people were expecting violence. We chose one far up a mountain, a very rough twenty-seven kilometers from the paved "Friendship Road" that runs past the base of Mount Everest into China. Except for police and international observers, all vehicle traffic was prohibited throughout Nepal that day. Twelve million people—some of them more than a hundred years old!—walked to the polls to cast their ballots for the first time. When I asked one 103-year-old how she made it up the mountain to vote, she explained that her son had carried her. The Maoists kept their promise and, surprisingly, there was very little violence that day. Cheering and grand parties erupted all over the country when the polls closed at 5:00 in the evening.

As our plane took off for home, we took in a magnificent panorama, from Annapurna to Everest, which was waving its trademark plume of snow as we left it behind and flew out over India. Jimmy and Rosalynn Carter had been on an African tour before the Nepalese election, and were headed to an even greater challenge after it. They were part of a group of "Elders"—internationally prominent leaders—who had planned to travel to the Middle East for a peace effort. One by one the others had dropped out or were barred by the Israeli government, so that only the Carters remained. "I am determined to go ahead anyway," Jimmy told me as our plane approached Tel Aviv. "There can be no real peace for anyone in the Middle East until someone forces the door open to dialogue about what is being done to the Palestinians."

A great deal of controversy and some danger surrounded this trip, and I assured the Carters of my prayers for their success. I don't know any Christians anywhere in the world who work harder than Jimmy and Rosalynn Carter at loving their "enemies" and opening doors to dialogue and peace. Given all that they had endured in the previous two weeks, and the trial they were walking into, I was extremely moved that Jimmy listened intently to my renewed hopes for the North Korea project on that trip and offered his enthusiastic blessing.

It took more than a year of messages back and forth, but finally Han announced to us that his contacts in North Korea were ready to meet with a group of us face-to-face to discuss the proposed project. In July 2008, six of us—including David Snell from the Fuller Center and Scott Angle, dean of the University of Georgia's College of Agriculture and Environmental Studies, as well as two old Peace Corps Korea friends, Kevin O'Donnell (Kevin having been my boss in South Korea before moving on to Washington to become the worldwide Peace Corps director) and Richard MacIntyre—finally acquired our visas and flew to Pyongyang. Han Park led the way.

We were very much aware that this was an extraordinary breakthrough that was possible only because of the persistent efforts at trust-building by Han over many decades. This trip made close to fifty for him to North Korea. It was a great success, but we learned that the road ahead of us was very long and uphill. I had helped to start such projects in a number of other countries, but never had I sensed such a wide gap to be crossed—in trust, in culture, and even in assumptions about how to launch such an effort. We were bedeviled by the details at many points.

One key discovery that gave us all great hope, however, was that both sides shared the strong belief that peacemaking between our respective peoples is the most crucial element in this effort. Indeed, thanks again to Han Park's connections, our official host in North Korea was the Asia Pacific Peace Committee. Over and over the people we met emphasized the importance of trust-building and peace—and we were all convinced that the feelings were sincere.

Two years earlier, in July 2006, Typhoon Ewiniar had devastated North Korea, killing more than 10,000 people by some estimates and destroying about 30,000 homes. Even before that disaster, especially in rural villages, shelter was in short supply, and often two families had to share one small house. After Ewiniar, according to Han, it became common for three families to be crowded into the tiny homes in some of the villages.

North Korea's winters are bitterly cold, with storms originating in the Arctic sweeping in from across Siberia. Few villages have enough wood or other fuel for heat, and houses are generally poorly insulated. Even with their heroic determination and *Juche* spirit, the people of rural North Korea are severely tested by such conditions. From the beginning, we stressed that we were interested only in building houses for these villagers—not the people, officials or otherwise, who lived in the capital city of Pyongyang. Our hosts quickly agreed with this condition.

Our effort suffered a tragic setback when our staunch supporter Millard Fuller died quite suddenly in February 2009. Linda said at the time, "Millard would not want people to mourn his death. He would be more interested in having people put on a tool belt and build a house for people in need." We agreed and felt the best way to honor our dear friend was to push ahead with the North Korea project.

In November 2009, four of us returned for the event toward which we had been working for years: the official groundbreaking. We didn't know as we flew over the sea from Beijing into Pyongyang on November 10 the drama that was playing out below us between North and South Korean gunboats. A disputed maritime border has been a volatile source of tension for decades, but the clash of the two navies was the first violent skirmish in seven years, with each side accusing the other of violating territorial waters. When we heard this news, I felt gratitude that we were on a mission to contribute at least a small push in the direction of peacemaking and trust.

On Wednesday, November 11, we drove out to the proposed building site at Osan-ri, near the Pyongyang airport. The cooperatively farmed tree nursery surrounding it—contributing to much-needed reforestation in the country—provided an ideal setting to showcase our small gesture of Korean-American friendship. About fifty farmers, mostly men, stood waiting in rows, dressed in their best black clothes.

I pictured the twenty-five duplexes, each with two living spaces of about 750 square feet apiece, rising up on that hillside. Already many of the sites had been leveled and the boundaries of the foundations marked. Standing under a banner announcing in both Korean and English "Groundbreaking Ceremony for 50 Dwellings for Farmers, 2009.11.11," we shared a ceremony of celebration and symbolically shoveled the first spades of dirt.

The Paektusan Academy of Architecture will help manage the project, and professionals from the United States and North Korea will work together to develop house plans that are energy efficient and environmentally sensitive in their construction and maintenance. I plan to lead the first few teams of volunteers from the United States and other countries, which will work side by side with Koreans to build the houses—and, we hope, trust. "We may not change international relations by this venture," said David Snell, "but we will provide the opportunity for Koreans and Americans to come together for good and to get to know one another as fellow travelers and trusted friends."

I enjoyed the ceremony, but the high point for me came right afterward. I broke away from the other "dignitaries" representing the North Korean government and the Fuller Center and waded into the crowd of farmers and laborers. The stunned looks on their faces seemed to communicate that seeing an American this close was a new experience for them. With a little effort, I found a man who spoke English, and with his help, I shared how much I looked forward to working with them on this project.

When I finished, in one great motion the crowd closed in

around me, smiling broadly. Han joined us and began to joke affectionately with the farmers. At one point he asked them something, and they all stared at me and then laughed. Han explained, "I asked them to guess how old you are—and then I told them." They were surprised to learn my age; apparently seventy years of life in North Korea takes a more visible toll than it does in the United States.

I wished at that moment that all the world had eyes to perceive this startling—and months ago seemingly impossible—vision come to life in such a beautiful but isolated corner of the world. God is indeed doing a new thing!

Back home, on the other side of the globe, people all across the United States were laying wreaths and singing patriotic songs in commemoration of Veterans Day, remembering the bravery of those who have fought and sacrificed their lives in our many wars. I longed for the day when those of us committed to waging peace are willing to do so with as much passion and courage and persistence. On that North Korean hillside, under the beaming sun, I saw a glimmer of possibility. I still get a thrill of excitement when I think of that comforting wall of smiling North Koreans encircling me, and my promise to them as I left: "I'll be back soon!"

Epilogue:
Action and Reaction

Years ago Carolyn and I were driving along the Mississippi River in Kentucky. We decided to visit some of the ancient mounds built a thousand years ago by the Native Americans of the area. We joined a cluster of other tourists on a walking tour led by an energetic young man who had grown up on a nearby farm.

We remember very little about the archaeological wonders we saw that day, but the guide made an indelible impression. He clearly had not spent much of his life in a classroom, but that didn't matter. He was so eager to share each of the marvels with us that we began to catch his enthusiasm as we followed him through the excavations.

Then, eyes glowing with anticipation, he led us into a dimly lit room of the visitors' center for the grand finale. He had us line up facing a large glass case. With a proud flourish, he leaned over and turned on an ultraviolet light. Instantly an array of fluorescent minerals in the case glowed brightly in a rainbow of beautiful colors.

"Now ya see that?" he asked. "Ya may be wondrin' what makes 'em shine like 'at. I'll tell you. Hit ain't nothin' but action and reaction. That's all it is—action and reaction."

Ever since that tour, Carolyn and I have fallen back on our young guide's all-purpose explanation when we have observed a mysterious phenomenon or a surprising groundswell of response to some idea or incident. "Hit ain't nothin' but action and reaction!"

In his book *The Tipping Point,* Malcolm Gladwell talks about "action and reaction" in a somewhat more sophisticated way. Gladwell argues that "ideas and products and messages and behaviors spread like viruses do."[1] This is true, he says, whether the ideas are good or bad, beneficial or destructive. Given the right circumstances, usually with one or more vigorous communicators at work, some ideas are capable of being spread until the "tipping point" is reached—the level at which the momentum for change becomes unstoppable.

Jesus was the quintessential communicator, whose teachings were reinforced by his actions. In his last days, even while looking out over the city of Jerusalem and weeping for its sorrow, he taught his followers that life is a precious creation of God, imbued with love and beauty. He called us to follow his example, constantly working to tip the balance away from evil and the suffering it causes toward good. He rejected both denial ("How is it you cannot interpret this fateful hour?" [Luke 12:56, NEB]) and despair ("Do not be afraid; only have faith" [Mark 5:36, NEB]).

Jesus called us to wake up to "the things that make for peace"—and put them into action. His love never faltered, even as he was being nailed to the cross. As a result, his message spread throughout the world. Not only did it sweep over the seemingly omnipotent Roman Empire, but it also provided a powerful new way to disarm all violent systems and ways of living.

For almost two centuries, the early followers of Jesus refused to take up arms against their enemies. Instead, ready to die for their faith, they spread the message of God's love. For every one who was martyred, new converts were won by their example. The gospel became, well, "unstoppable."

And yet, how dull we are! Century after century, we set aside Jesus' example, go out to destroy our enemies rather than love them, and then intone his words, "Forgive us the wrong we have done, as we have forgiven those who have wronged us" (Matthew 5:12, NEB), as we bury our dead and prepare to go out for yet another round of war.

Knowing how prone we are to mistake pious words for faithful action, Jesus stressed again and again that words and action are totally different. He ended the most famous sermon in history by asserting, "Not everyone who calls me 'Lord, Lord' will enter the kingdom of Heaven, but only those who *do* the will of my heavenly Father" (Matthew 7:21, NEB; emphasis added).

When I arrived at Koinonia Partners, just a few months after Clarence Jordan's death, I found a dusty box of old reel-to-reel tape and wire recordings in the little study shack where he had suffered his fatal heart attack. I listened to them hour after hour. Later I edited a number of them, and we offered them for sale through our Koinonia newsletter.

My favorite was Clarence's reflections on the Sermon on the Mount, which grew into a book he authored by the same name. It was Jesus' most well-known sermon that had changed Clarence's life when he was a young man in ROTC (Reserve Officers Training Corps) at the University of Georgia. One summer day, just days away from being commissioned as a second lieutenant in the U.S. Cavalry, he sat on a black horse, pistol in one hand and saber in the other.

When his turn came to gallop through the woods, stabbing and shooting at straw dummies, one verse of the sermon kept repeating itself in Clarence's mind: "But I say to you, love your enemies..." (Matthew 5:44). At the end of that drill, Clarence walked over to his commanding officer and announced that he was resigning his commission. From that day on, he set his sights on becoming a preacher.

Clarence called the Sermon on the Mount the "platform of the God Movement," whose purpose was "not to evoke inspiration but perspiration."[2] He liked ending his sermons as Jesus ended his, with the parable found in the concluding verses of Matthew 7. There are two types of Christians, said Clarence. The one who hears and *does* the Word of God is like a wise man who builds his house on a rock, with a foundation sturdy enough to survive through wind and floods. The person who hears the Word of God but doesn't do it, according to Clarence, is like the foolish man who builds his house on sand, with a foundation that collapses as soon as the wind whips up and the waters rise. Clarence ended his reflections on this parable with the command, "Now let us go forth to classify ourselves."[3]

I saw a dramatic example of what can happen when the tipping point is triggered and large numbers of people into a movement of "loving their enemies." In the fall of 2002, it was still unclear whether I was going to be jailed or punished in some other way for taking medicine to the children in Iraq. Rather than allow ourselves to be paralyzed by that uncertainty, we at Jubilee continued working for an end to the broad sanctions our nation had imposed against that country. We also raised more money for additional shipments of medicine to the children. By the end of the year, we had enough for another eight or ten truckloads.

Dr. Robert Edgar, who was the general secretary of the National Council of Churches (NCC), invited me to participate in a conference call of Christian peace activists who were concerned about the growing momentum toward another invasion of Iraq. I told the others about Jubilee's work against the sanctions and proposed that there be a broader effort by a consortium of organizations willing to join us. Soon thereafter, several of us met in Washington, D.C., and founded the All Our Children campaign.

The NCC, Church World Service, Mennonite Central Committee, Lutheran World Relief, Sojourners, and the Stop Hunger Campaign joined Jubilee Partners as official sponsors of the effort. We were fairly optimistic that a coalition of organizations representing fully a quarter of the U.S. public could get a permit from our government to ship the medicine, but most of us agreed that we would move ahead with the action with or without such permission. In fact, the permit was granted in record time!

A short time later, I joined Bob on a special delegation sponsored by the NCC. A dozen of us, most of the others prominent church leaders, went to Baghdad in a final effort to help head off the war that now seemed all but inevitable. We had meetings with Iraq's religious leaders, Christian and Muslim. We visited hospitals, attended church services, and spoke at press conferences.

An hour before midnight on December 31, 2002, we joined the members of the Evangelical Presbyterian Church in central Baghdad to share the final hour of the year with them. The service was interrupted for a few minutes as we were invited to circulate through the church to be greeted by the members. One elderly man said to me with tears in his eyes, "I know your country's bombs will be falling on us very soon, maybe within a month, but I love you. You are my Christian brother. Thank you for coming to Baghdad." He shook my hand vigorously and then hugged me tightly.

When we returned to our seats at the front of the church, the platform was filled with beautiful children, aged about 10 to 12. Each of them wore a long-sleeved sweater with a satin cross stitched in the middle. For the next half hour these kids sang one song after another. Most of the songs were in English, obviously prepared especially for their guests from the United States. I was absolutely charmed by them.

It turned out that my elderly friend's prediction was off by only a few weeks. On March 19 the aerial attack began. For the next two weeks, bombers and cruise missiles pounded Baghdad unmercifully in the U.S.-sponsored "shock and awe" campaign. I imagined the screams of the children who had sung for us "Lord, I Lift Your Name on High" just a short time earlier, and I felt almost as though I were the one being attacked. In one news video from Baghdad, I was horrified to see a huge cloud of flame rising right from the neighborhood where we had worshiped together in the Presbyterian church.

Bob Edgar and I visited with Jimmy and Rosalynn Carter shortly after our return from Iraq. They had been in Norway less than a month earlier, where he had received the Nobel Peace

Prize. They quickly agreed to help us promote All Our Children. They issued a statement that said in part, "We urge all people of compassion to join in supporting the All Our Children campaign. The immediate goal is to provide emergency medical supplies to save thousands of Iraqi children who are victims of an international situation for which they have no responsibility."

As the weeks passed—full as they were of tragic news from the war in Iraq—it was clear that we had indeed reached a tipping point with some good news. I traveled around the country to help promote the campaign. Wherever I went, I saw notices in church bulletins and posters in their foyers calling on people to join this compassionate alternative to violence against our "enemies." Churches all over the world responded with help for the Iraqi children. Some mosques also joined in, as did people from numerous secular groups that wanted desperately to do *something* to help the children.

"Hit's action and reaction for sure!" Carolyn and I observed happily.

By September, we were already approaching the million-dollar limit that we had been allowed. We stretched our funds by purchasing supplies from less expensive sources abroad, accepted big in-kind donations, and relied on volunteer help whenever possible. Consequently, we were able to more than double the amount of aid actually provided. The medicine and supplies went to an estimated 200,000 children and more than 50,000 adults. Hospital facilities were expanded and improved to serve an estimated 60,000 additional children each year.

The love and goodwill conveyed through these tangible gifts were priceless. As I watched all this unfold, one of the things that began to give me the most hope was the way people do respond with compassion once they finally find ways to get beyond their fears and stereotypes and have a clear way to act on their concern.

I thought of all the remarkable events Carolyn and I had witnessed around that same time: the deliverance of Ron Thomas and me from a would-be assassination squad in Bany Mohammed

Sha'rawy; the experience of building a house for a poor Arab family in north Jordan while Israeli jets flew overhead to attack Syria; the outpouring of gratitude from the Jordanian people at the end of that dramatic week. Over and over we see miracles happen right before our eyes. And still we usually seem unable to grasp the full significance of what has happened, to remember it, or to learn from it and then to act on it—or, as the prophet Isaiah urged, to "shout it from the mountaintop"!

What makes us so stubbornly, incredibly, unbelievably dull? Perhaps at least part of the answer is being discovered by scientists in the field of neuropsychiatry. Aided by new technologies involving MRIs and PET scans, scientists are able to map very precisely which regions of the brain are involved in fear, love, the use of abstract symbols, and so on.

One discovery is that of the so-called "reptilian brain," that central region of the human brain that reacts to perceived threats in very nearly the same way as the brains of lizards, snakes, or alligators. Its sole focus seems to be on survival. Abstractions are handled by a different part of the brain, as are the more complex emotions that make us uniquely human. Above all else, the business of the "reptilian" part of our brain is self-preservation.

We like to think of ourselves, in the words of the psalmist, as created "a little lower than the angels." In reality, however, we spend much of our time acting as though we are only a little above the reptiles. We'd probably have something closer to an appropriate level of humility if we thought of our brains as cobbled together out of children's Tinker Toys™ or Legos™, rather than thinking of ourselves as semi-celestial beings. Too often we allow ourselves to be controlled by fear, narrowing our options to fight-or-flight, attack-or-run.

Jesus called us to move beyond such primitive instincts and behaviors. Fear, when we give it too much power, shuts down our ability to reach out to others in love. We lose the ability to feel empathy and compassion for others, to see situations through their eyes. To be peacemakers. Worse still, we tend too often to stare right at God's marvelous work among us and then sleepwalk along our way without having grasped the significance of what we have seen.

Jesus reminded his followers of Isaiah's words about hearing and looking without understanding, about minds that have become dull. Decades later in Rome, in the very last passages of the book of Acts, Paul was still quoting the very same words to his skeptical audience in Rome. And here we are, twenty centuries later...

Dear God, please don't give up on us!

One thing has become very clear to me through the experiences described in this book: Nothing overcomes the paralysis of fear or the dullness of mind better than going out and acting on our faith. Even the smallest step, taken in love, clears our vision enough so that we can see to take another step toward God's emerging will for us. And then another.

When we put down our weapons and look for ways to reach out to those we perceive as enemies—to love them and return good for evil, refusing to be controlled by fear—we discover new options that were simply not visible to us before. Most important, as we stumble along as best we can, we will find that we have indeed acted our way into a new way of thinking. *We will discover that God really is right there with us.* And literally nothing else in all creation—not even the most dangerous situations, or the greatest challenges facing humankind—*nothing* matters more than that!

Isaiah urges us to shout the good news from the mountaintop, "Your God is here!" When we grasp that wonderful truth, the prophet promises that, no matter how weary we may become in the struggle, we will overcome our fear, find new strength, and "mount up with wings like eagles." Claiming that strength, we can soar to heights where all borders disappear and only beauty remains.

Notes

Introduction

1. Joyce Hollyday, ed. *Clarence Jordan: Essential Writings* (Maryknoll, NY: Orbis Books, 2003), 143.
2. Ibid., 31.
3. Ibid., 143.

Chapter 3: No Time to Waste

1. Lester R. Brown, "Starving the People to Feed the Cars," *The Washington Post,* September 10, 2006.
2. Lester R. Brown, *Plan B 3.0: Mobilizing to Save Civilization* (New York: W. W. Norton, 2008).
3. Gwynne Dyer, *Climate Wars* (Victoria, Australia: Scribe Publications, 2008), xiii.

Chapter 4: Aid and Comfort

1. "The Health Conditions of the Population in Iraq Since the Gulf Crisis." www.who.int/disasters/repo/5249.html.
2. "Middle East UN Official Blasts Iraq Sanctions." September 30, 1998. http://news.bbc.co.uk/2/hi/183499.stm.

Chapter 5: I'm Not Lost from God

1. Robert W. McChesney, *The Problem of the Media* (New York: Monthly Review Press, 2004), 72-74.
2. Samuel P. Huntington, *The Clash of Civilizations and the Remaking of World Order* (New York: Simon and Schuster, 1996), 21.
3. Ibid., 212.
4. Ibid., 213-14.
5. Greg Mortenson and David Oliver Relin, *Three Cups of Tea* (New York: Penguin Books, 2007), 294-95.
6. Oscar Romero, *The Violence of Love* (Farmington, PA: Plough Publishing House, 2007), 39.

Chapter 7: Groundbreaking Faith

1. Dr. Han S. Park's ideas are explained in great detail in his book *North Korea: The Politics of Unconventional Wisdom* (Lynne Reinner Publishers, Inc., 2002).

Epilogue

1. Malcolm Gladwell, *The Tipping Point* (Boston: Little, Brown, & Co., 2002), 7.
2. Joyce Hollyday, ed. *Clarence Jordan: Essential Writings,* 31.
3. Ibid., 32.